The Creative Writer

Level Four: Becoming a Writer

Publisher's Cataloging-In-Publication Data
(Prepared by The Donohue Group, Inc.)

Fishman, Boris, 1979-
    The creative writer. Level four, Becoming a writer / by Boris Fishman.

    p. : ill. ; cm.

    "... designed to be used in a mentor/student relationship, with teaching, guidance, and evaluation tips provided
for the mentor or teacher."--Publisher's e-mail communication.
    Interest grade level: 5-8.
    ISBN: 978-1-933339-63-4

    1. Creative writing (Elementary education) 2. Creative writing (Middle school) 3. English language--
Composition and exercises--Study and teaching (Elementary) 4. English language--Composition and exercises--
Study and teaching (Middle school) I. Title. II. Title: Becoming a writer

LB1576 .F571 2013
372.62/3
2012923239

For a complete list of history, grammar, reading, and writing materials produced by Peace Hill Press,
or to request a catalog, visit **peacehillpress.com**.

The Creative Writer

Level Four: Becoming a Writer

by Boris Fishman

PEACE HILL PRESS
CHARLES CITY, VA

PREFACE

Whether you've been with *The Creative Writer* series from Level One or you're picking it up for the first time, you're about to embark on the most exciting part of the ride. *The Creative Writer, Level Four: Becoming a Writer* reviews the skills covered in Levels One through Three and introduces new, more advanced ones. It also offers guidance on the writing life: How to find time to write during a busy schedule; how to maintain discipline; how to deal with rejection; how to submit to literary journals.

That last will be the goal you'll be working toward all year: A story and poem polished enough to submit to a literary journal.

In the opening weeks, just as in previous levels of the series, we'll review what we've learned so far. Then we'll move on to new skills. As always, the first 18 weeks will be devoted to fiction, and the next 18 to poetry. Each lesson proceeds in the same style as previous levels of this series: A discussion of the week's subject is followed by an exercise (sometimes in several parts), followed by a challenge exercise should you wish to push yourself further.

Unlike previous levels, Level Four does not have a separate section of guidance for your mentor. By this point, you're ready to act like a writer--which means that you're ready to work on your own. But don't forget that all writers need editors. When you work on a project for days, weeks, or even months, you get so close to it that you lose sight of its flaws. You need a sympathetic outside reader to help you make a good piece of work even better.

A NOTE TO MENTORS:

By this point, the writer has developed sufficiently to grasp the relevant craft concepts, and make use of brainstorming guidance, largely on his or her own. But that doesn't mean the mentor is no longer useful. My hope is that mentors will read and use this book alongside their charges. Some writers prefer to work in solitude, but some, and beginning ones especially, can use soundboards.

Even though writers typically don't like others coming in and meddling with their ideas or prose, editors are indispensable. In order to achieve true understanding of their material, writers must get *very* familiar with it. (I spent three years on the novel I've just finished, hardly the longest time ever spent on a novel. In that time, I've come to know my characters better than my own family, and can recite significant portions of the novel by heart. You get *close*.) But the closer a writer gets, the less objective his or her eyes become; the writer *needs* that outside eye, supportive but fair, that can discern immediately whether something sounds false, unbelievable, or plain awkward.

For parents and teachers: This level is intended for more mature student writers, and the reading selections reflect this. If you are working with a younger student, please preview the student's assigned readings.

One more thing: Plan ahead. In the fiction section, Weeks 12, 15, and 17 will require the writer to visit the library; so might Week 14 of the poetry section.

TABLE OF CONTENTS

Fiction

Poetry

POETRY SECTION 4: FORMS

POETRY SECTION 5: NONSENSE

POETRY SECTION 6: FAVORITE POET

POETRY SECTION 7: ENLARGING OUR WORLD/POETRY AS A PUBLIC EXERCISE

CONCLUSION

FICTION

INTRODUCTION

REFRESHER

Purpose: To review skills developed in Levels One—Three.

If you worked on the previous levels of this series and someone asked you to describe, in as few words as possible, what they taught you, what would you say?

In thinking of the answer, I hope you remembered the Holy Grail, the answer to all questions! That's right: The 5 Essentials.

1. Plot
2. Characters
3. Dialogue
4. Point of view
5. Setting

A story needs something to happen. (**Plot.**) It needs **characters**. Presumably, those characters will have things to say to each other. (**Dialogue.**) You'll have to figure out who's telling the story. (**Point of view.**) And where it takes place. (**Setting.**)

This week, you're going to come up with these basic aspects of a new short story. First, I'll ask you to come up with a one-sentence **story idea**. Then, I'll ask you to develop it into a paragraph-long summary of what happens in the story. (One of these two first steps will probably involve you figuring out *where* the story is taking place.) You'll need to come up with brief profiles for each of the characters in the story, and also fill a page of your notebook with sample dialogue between them. Finally—though perhaps you'll end up figuring this out sooner—you'll need to decide who's telling the story.

So, step-by-step, here's what you need to do. (I'd suggest reading all the way through the next six points, down to the assignment summary, before you start working.)

1. COME UP WITH A ONE-SENTENCE SHORT STORY IDEA. (TWO SENTENCES WOULD BE FINE, TOO.)

Lots of things can make a story interesting or memorable—an irresistible lead character, a beautiful writing style, an atmosphere so realistic you can feel it in your bones—but in terms of plot, the best way to get the reader to turn the page is to make him wonder what happens next. That's called **suspense**. So, make sure your story idea is something that will make a listener (you can try it out on your mentor) say, "Hm, I wonder how that will turn out."

Examples:
  A. A group of friends goes to a secluded lake cabin that turns out to be haunted.
  B. Lily and Cassandra are each other's only friends. Cassandra's father has to move the family for work.
  C. No one in the town of Wortham speaks.

Let's put these story ideas to the "I wonder what will happen next" test. **Story Idea A** is a classic horror-movie setup, and if horror movies know how to do one thing, it's how to keep you on the edge of your seat. You have no idea who the main characters are yet, but aren't you dying to find out what happens at the cursed lake cabin? (Later this year, we'll practice writing horror stories.)

Story Idea B plays with a different kind of suspense. How will Lily—and Cassandra—deal with the other's disappearance from her life?

Story Idea C sounds like a slightly fantastical story. The premise—that no one in town speaks—makes me think that something is going to happen to challenge this age-old fact (a mysterious new arrival? some kind of natural catastrophe?). Something is going to make this town start speaking, and the suspense is in what is going to ensue when it does. Or: The suspense could be in what made this town fall silent in the first place, a mystery that some new arrival in town has to solve before being able to move forward in his journey.

2. EXPAND THE STORY IDEA INTO A PLOT.

Many authors don't like this step. They say that you shouldn't overplan what's ahead—you should figure it out as you go. The great novelist E. L. Doctorow has a saying to this effect: Writing a novel is like driving at night: You can see only as far as the headlights illuminate, but you can make the whole journey that way. In other words, you only need to know what happens next, and you can worry about what happens after that when you get there.

Some authors can work this way, but just as many plan out—at least in general—what their story or novel will be about. That's what I want you to do here. Give me one paragraph of several sentences expanding the one- or two-sentence story idea. For example, using Story Idea B:

> "The story opens with a girl named Cassandra having to leave her beloved friend Lily because her—Cassandra's—father has to move cities for work. After Cassandra arrives at her destination, she and Lily hatch a plan to run away from their homes and meet in some third place, where they will live together, without the adults. Despite difficulties and danger, they reach each other, only to find that as 11-year-olds, they have no means to live on their own, away from the adults."

Alternative:

> "The story opens with Lily, a lonely girl in Town X. Lily has no friends because she's shy and awkward. Soon, Cassandra moves in next door. Cassandra is a misfit, too, but for the opposite reason: She's brash and explosive. In fact, that's why her family has had to move—she was kicked out of her previous school. Somehow, these two odd ducks are just right for each other, and, through a series of experiences, become the best of friends. But their joy at having found the other comes to an abrupt end when Cassandra's family has to move yet again, this time because her father, who hasn't been able to find a job in Town X, receives one elsewhere."

Notes:

Before we proceed with this week's assignment, an aside about some details in the example above:

Note how different the stories above are. In one, the separation happens at the beginning and in the other, at the end. The story that separates the girls at the beginning places less **emphasis** on why they're so close—the story essentially asks the reader to take it for granted—and **more** emphasis on what they will do to remain close. The story that separates the girls at the end does the opposite: By spending the whole story providing examples of—in other words, **showing**—what has made the girls so tight—the revelation at story's end that the girls will have to separate is meant to strike the reader like an anvil to the heart.

What you have here are different **structures** for a story about the close friendship of two girls. As you can see, different structures can lead the story in very different directions.

Emphasis is critical within stories, too. The first story idea might choose to spend time on how the two girls got to the destination they escape to, or it might choose to skip over that in order to focus on what happens to them when they get there. Or it might detail both. Everything depends on what the author is trying to say. The author can emphasize the depth of the girls' friendship by focusing on everything they went through to be together, or on everything they endure after they meet.

Note as well that the **alternative** plot comes up with brief **character** sketches for the girls.

3. CHARACTERS

Let's stick with Lily and Cassandra. What is each like? Are they similar or different? What do they like about each other? Why don't they have any other friends? What kind of adjectives would describe them? Imagine each separately in the same situation; how would each act? List their likes and dislikes. These are some of the questions I'd try to answer in order to get a better handle on the girls.

Then I'd have to decide whether anyone else will play a large role in the story. Will the parents be major characters or just background noise because the true focus of the story will be Lily and Cassandra?

To sum up: Write a few sentences describing Lily and Cassandra—say, 50 to 100 words each. Then describe any other major characters using at least one or two sentences.

4. DIALOGUE

If I've done a good job with Essential 3, my dialogue will reflect the personalities of the girls. So, if Lily is shy and Cassandra is brash, a brief exchange might go like this (note that surrounding details accompany the dialogue; I'm imagining a whole scene):

As they approached the overgrown garden, the elephant ears of the squash swaying lightly in the hot wind, Lily reached up and took Cassandra's hand. Cassandra let her keep it there, though she didn't like holding hands, not with her mother, not with anyone. But if she had to do it with someone, she minded it least with Lily. When they got in the garden, Cassandra took off for the long row of tomatoes, which looked like pinpricks of blood on the great blue-green hide of the garden. When Cassandra took her hand away so she could tear the tomatoes off the vine, Lily moved her hands to the hem of Cassandra's t-shirt.

"You want to stay long?" Lily asked, her face pale.

Cassandra peeled herself away from the tomatoes. "What's *with* you?"

"Nothing," Lily rushed to say . "I've never been here before, you know."

"You've never come to the garden your daddy keeps?"' Cassandra said.

"So what?" Lily said.

Cassandra considered Lily for a long moment. "So you've been missing these tomatoes," she said, and, grinning, smashed a half-eaten tomato into Lily's nose, squirting juice down her shirt. Lily's eyes got big, her lips twitching. Then she noticed an overripe tomato next to her foot. She snatched it and slammed it into Cassandra's nose, though she got her cheek instead, splattering seeds everywhere. The girls stared at each other for a moment and exploded into laughter. They rolled around the baked earth and squealed, the big elephant ears swaying like bearded giants above them.

The segment above is only about 250 words, and only about a quarter of them are pure dialogue, but I needed to draw a **scene** in order come up with ideas for the dialogue. I'd gotten it into my mind (from my alternative plot idea above) that Lily is shy and Cassandra bold, so I asked myself what kind of scene could demonstrate that. Then I remembered wandering one dusky evening into a family garden on a farm where I was volunteering; it was so large and thick with vegetables that it felt nearly impenetrable in the gathering twilight, and a little frightening, too (for a countryside novice, at least). So I decided to make Lily frightened of the garden and Cassandra not. But I also wanted the experience to end up bringing them together rather than dividing them. And that's when the dialogue started to flow.

That's your task: Think of a scene, and start describing it. Your dialogue should flow from there. Aim for 250 words total, at least. Don't worry about whether or not the scene will end up in your story—just concentrate on letting your characters speak.

5. POINT OF VIEW

Refresher: First-person narratives have an "I" narrator, who is usually part of the story. Third-person narratives have a narrator who refers to all the characters as "he," "she," or "they," and may or may not be part of the story.

As you can see in the **dialogue** exercise above, I went with a third-person narrator, I think because this isn't Lily's or Cassandra's story—it's about them both, and it felt like it should be told by a third party. (Whether that third party is someone off-stage, or perhaps one of the girls' parents—that's one more choice to make.) You would have a different story if Lily was telling it, and different again if Cassandra was. None of these approaches is right or wrong; they would just lead to different stories, and you might have to try more than one before you find what works. In the novel I recently finished (which I revised 12 times), I started in the first-person ("I work at a magazine"). Somewhere around Draft 4, I changed to third-person ("Slava works at a magazine"). Several drafts later, I went back to first. And for Draft 10, I switched yet again. Writing isn't a science. Your understanding of the work evolves, and so do your creative decisions.

So now finish this step: Write down which point of view the story will use—and, if appropriate, who is narrating it.

6. SETTING

Where is this story taking place and is setting important? It's up to the author. I might choose to specify where the girls are located (that Cassandra says "daddy" rather than "dad" or "father" makes me think we're in the South; the garden makes me think we're in a rural location), and where Cassandra's father has to relocate, and where the girls decide to run away to. But I might also choose to keep all these descriptions very general ("the farm," "the city") because it might be a way of universalizing this story. It wouldn't be only about these specific two girls in some specific place, then; it would be about everyone who's ever had to give up a friend.

All right, your turn. Write 50-100 words describing the setting.

Here's a summary of what you should accomplish in this lesson:

Your assignment: Following the cues above, come up with a story idea, expanded plot, characters, dialogue, point of view, and setting for a story of your choosing.

FICTION • SECTION 1

POINT OF VIEW

WEEKS 2 - 3

HEY, YOU!

Purpose: To learn more about second-person ("you") narration.

In our first section this year, we're going to practice doing more with point of view.

In earlier levels of this series, we practiced writing from the first-person and third-person points of view. Now it's time to consider how stories with second-person narrators work. Here's an example:

> You're not the kind of guy who would be at a place like this at this time of the morning.

(That's the opening line of a famous novel called *Bright Lights, Big City* by Jay McInerney.[1])

Why do authors use second-person? What does it give us?

In *Bright Lights, Big City*, the narrator is **narrating his own actions, or addressing himself**. But couldn't we achieve that with a first-person narrator? Let's see:

> I'm not the kind of guy who would be at a place like this at this time of the morning.

---

1 McInerney, Jay. *Bright Lights, Big City.* (New York, NY: Vintage Contemporaries, 1984), p. 1.

Don't the two sentences sound different? The first one is a little chiding, the second one a little defensive. Readers might disagree about which works "better," but you'll agree they suggest different feelings.

For me, there's something about the (imagined) split into two creatures that makes Jay McInerney's version, the second-person version, sound more believable and less precious. (Don't you often find yourself saying, for instance, "When you ask her for a break, she never agrees!" when you literally mean "When I ask her for a break, she never agrees"?) It's also a handy device for addressing younger or older versions of oneself. So you might call second-person a **device**—a gimmick—that enables authors to create characters who are narrating their own actions or addressing themselves.

But do they have to be? Couldn't they be **narrating the actions of, or addressing, some actual "you"**?

> By the time you read this, I'll be gone.

This sounds like a parent addressing a child, or a friend addressing another friend, or one half of a couple addressing the other. You might ask: But couldn't we achieve the same effect with a third-person narrator? Let's try it.

> By the time Marnie read his letter, he would be gone.

That's a completely different story! What started as a narrator's direct, immediate, intimate address of another character became a somewhat impersonal observation by some third-person narrator. And whereas we still don't know who Marnie is—daughter? wife?—the narrator is forced to say more about the "you" in this third-person version, whereas in the earlier example, he could keep that mystery going for as long as he wanted.

To me, third-person feels far less immediate and intimate. (On the other hand, it's less confining. A third-person narrator can see everything; a second-person narrator must usually focus on one person: "you," possibly in addition to him or herself.) There's also something creepy—effectively so—about narrating someone else's actions in second-person. If you're writing a horror story about someone spying on someone else, or a detective story about a private investigator constantly tailing a mark—any story involving a very intense, close relationship where observation by one party of another is key—second-person may be what you want.

A second-person narration doesn't have to narrate the activities of, or address, oneself or another. It could also **address the reader**. Here's the opening line from Italo Calvino's novel *If on a winter's night a traveler*:

> You are about to begin reading Italo Calvino's new novel *If on a winter's night a traveler*.[2]

How about that for direct? In my own novel as well, which is (currently!) written in third-person, the narrator periodically does what's known as "breaking the fourth wall"—that is, he breaks the wall between narrator and reader and addresses the reader directly. What advantage does this bring? It involves the reader more actively in the narrative. Imagine if Calvino opened his novel with:

> The reader is about to begin reading…

How stiff and formal this alternative seems by comparison, doesn't it?

It's important to note that few authors use second-person because it's so limiting, especially in novels—300 pages limited to an address of some "you," whether oneself, another character, or the reader, can come to feel very confining. But if your mission is to do any of those things, there's no device more effective than second-person.

Your assignment: In the three second-person-narrator examples above, "you" can refer to:
1. the narrator of the story
2. another character in the story, or
3. the reader.

Pick one and compose 500 words of a short story on any subject using that point of view. If you're flailing for an idea, use your idea from last week, only modified to

---

2 Calvino, Italo. *If on a winter's night a traveler*, trans. William Weaver. (New York, NY: Harcourt Brace Jovanovich, 1981), p.3.

second-person narration. (Using my example from last week, that might mean 500 words of Lily addressing Cassandra in a diary entry.) Don't worry about how unrealistic or unlikely the 500 words sound—you don't have to finish the story, so you can get your second-person narrator into all sorts of trouble!

CHALLENGE EXERCISE:

Do the same thing for the other two forms of address.

WHO, WE?

Purpose: To learn more about collective ("we"), or first-person plural, narration.

As you saw last week, switching to a second-person ("you") narrator from the more traditional first- and third-person gives the author some freedoms (and some restrictions, too). This week, we'll explore the fourth, and last, major point of view—the collective, or first-person plural, narration.

Collective narration refers to stories told by some kind of—you guessed it—collection of people. (These are distinct from stories with multiple narrators—that is, stories with one section told from one person's point of view, another from another's, and so on.) Collective narrators are almost as uncommon in fiction as second-person narrators, but many well-known authors have made use of them. Perhaps the best-known example of collective narration comes from William Faulkner's short story "A Rose for Emily," about a Southern town's relationship with a mysterious recluse in its midst, which opens this way:

> When Miss Emily Grierson died, our whole town went to her funeral.[3]

And here is the opening line from a more recent work of fiction, the novel *Then We Came to the End*, by Joshua Ferris, about employees of an advertising firm:

> We were fractious and overpaid.[4]

---

3 Faulkner, William. *Selected Short Stories*. Random House, 2012, p. 47.
4 Ferris, Joshua. *Then We Came to the End*. (New York, NY: Little, Brown and Co., 2007), p. 3.

(Do you know what "fractious" means? If not, look it up. Make that your habit throughout this volume. If you encounter a word you don't know, look it up, even if I don't explicitly instruct you to. You might want to devote a specific part of your notebook to this vocabulary list. This should be your practice outside this series as well: Any time you come across a word you don't know, whether in someone's speech or in a book, note it and look it up. And don't be afraid to ask people what the words they're using mean. No shame in not knowing—shame only in not asking!)

From these examples, what can we say about the kind of purpose and advantage collective narration serves? Joshua Ferris' novel is, in part, about the dehumanizing effects of corporate employment. And so, he brings to life this notion—that sometimes it's hard to feel like an individual in a corporate workplace—by taking away individuality from his narrator. In this way, his **form** mimics his **content**. **Content** refers to what the book says; **form** refers to how the book says it. So, Ferris echoes his content (a book about the dehumanizing effects of the workplace) in his form (a story told from the perspective of a collective narrator, not an individual with character and personality and *humanity*).

William Faulkner chooses the collective narrator for symbolic reasons as well. "A Rose for Emily" touches on the power of conformity—the enforcement of like-minded thinking—in places like Faulkner's rural South. So if you're writing a story about something having to do with individuals vs. the group, you might consider a collective narrator.

"We" narrators can serve other purposes as well. Have you ever read a Greek play? You might remember the presence of a Greek chorus, or a collective voice that offers a commentary on the play's events. The chorus can be involved in the story's events, or not; it can serve as a voice of reason, or of herd mentality. The options are many— it all depends on what you're trying to achieve.

But does a collective narrator offer any advantages in terms of craft? Let's take one of the sentences above and re-write it as both first-person and third-person sentences:

Original: "We were fractious and overpaid."

First: "I was fractious and overpaid."

Third: "They were fractious and overpaid."

What do we think? All three approaches have their value, but each comes at the story from a very different perspective. What do collective narrators have that other narrators don't? If you said anything like, "Well, they're collective," you're right. They have the power of numbers. A number of voices has greater authority than a single one. It may be an unhealthy kind of authority, so perhaps we should say "power" instead of "authority."

Collective narration is sleight of hand: It gives only the *illusion* of many voices. If you read any of the stories/novels mentioned above, you'll see that the collective voice speaks in unison; it doesn't squabble within itself. That's the trick: Collective narration makes it sound as if the story carries with it the power of many, but the uniformity of opinion of one.

Are you ready to try your hand at creating a collective narrator? This week's **assignment** is to write 500 words of a short story from the perspective of a group. The 500 words could consist of pure narration, or it could contain a combination of narration and scene, and even dialogue. However, it might seem funny to write things like "'No, thank you,' we said." Whenever collective narrators enter the action, they tend to do so not in a group speaking in unison (unless we're talking about a Greek chorus), but via one of its members, though his experiences continue to be narrated from the group's perspective. ("When Josiah, the old farmer by Huppert Pond, rose to speak, we stood behind him. 'Settle down, now,' he said.") It's as if the narration briefly switches to third-person.

Below is a short example of collective narration by me, followed by an analysis. After reading it, try your hand at your own.

> So what if we don't stay here year-round, or we started buying homes
> around here only in the last generation? That means we don't have a say at

all, or half a say? Our pipes freeze, and our roses get chewed up by the deer, too: This is our place as much as anyone's.

But when Telco Gas came offering to dig up half the earth in town in exchange for a couple of checks, Duke Jenner, his red hunting cap askew, got up at the town hall and said what was on everyone's mind, anyway: "Nobody who don't live here full-time gets a say." Well, that was when the wheels came off. We? We weren't going to let that go by without comment. Now it was out in the open. Now, we would do something about it.

Analysis: What do you make of this story opening? It seems to pit two camps: Old-timers and newcomers to a (so-far) unnamed town. The newcomers are narrating the story and doing so from a collective perspective. Their camp consists of individuals, of course, but the old-timers tend to see them as one undifferentiated group—the newcomers—and so the story brings that to life through collective narration. (Of course, you could have an individual narrating a story about the very same thing—it would simply read and feel differently.)

Your turn.

Your assignment. Write 500 words from the perspective of a collective narrator. Your first step should be no different from any other story excerpt, except you might spend a little time thinking about story ideas involving groups. What's a group? These are all groups:

- The cool kids at school
- The adults
- The animals in the woods
- The gods of Greek mythology
- The day laborers in town

Then you might think about what kind of story idea would take advantage of their perspective as a group rather than as individuals. Previously, I've encouraged you to individualize your characters as much as possible, to make them as unique and complex as real-life people. Collective narration allows us to do the opposite—to highlight an entire group's preoccupations, for better or worse. And so if you wanted to write a story about what it's like to be a strawberry-picker from Mexico in a mostly white town, you could do it through a story about the friendship between an individual Mexican migrant and an individual "townie" (with a first- or third-person narrator) or through a collective narration where the narration is done either by the "Mexican migrants in town" or "the townies." This collective story still needs as distinct a plot as any other, but the collective narration allows an author to talk about a group's experience without resorting to generalizations, which never work well in any kind of writing.

CHALLENGE EXERCISE:

Are you interested in reading more collective narration? Check out these titles in the library:

- *The Virgin Suicides*, by Jeffrey Eugenides
- *During the Reign of the Queen of Persia*, by Joan Chase
- *Our Kind*, by Kate Walbert

FICTION • SECTION 2

WORD CHOICE

WEEKS 4 - 5

THE THESAURUS EXERCISE

Purpose: To expand our vocabulary.

Those of you who have been with this series since the first volume may remember an exercise called "If I could count the ways," which asked you to write the same sentence 10 different ways. This exercise is similar, but I wanted to include it as this series' version of the pencil markings parents make on doorjambs to measure how much their kids have grown. In other words, I want you to see your progress. If you have Level One, go back after you've done this exercise, and compare your work then to your work now.

But let's back up. What are we doing this week? Once more, we'll practice ways of saying the same thing in different ways.

Why? Especially in a long project, it becomes really important for an author not to use the same words and phrases over and over. (Certain actions—"erupted in laughter," "droned on," "fell silent" —have a way of creeping into a novel over and over.) This is because no "eruption" of laughter is like another, and deserves to be described specifically rather than generically. Also, repetitive writing is not very fun for readers!

Good writers constantly work on expanding their language skills, imagination, and instincts. They do so by reading a lot (and not only fiction) and practicing their writing a lot. As many teachers of writing will tell you, you can't "study for" originality; you can only prepare for it to visit you, your laptop or notebook open in front of you, by practicing over and over.

A thesaurus can be great—when all you can think of is "frustration," it can help you realize that the word you're actually looking for—the thing your character is *actually* feeling—is "chagrin." But I don't know any writers who study vocabulary cards. It's fun and useful to learn new words, but it's overkill to make it a mission because then, inevitably, your short story is going to be full of words like "gormless" and "pietistic." And that sounds very mannered—not to mention alienating to the reader. Sixty-four dollar words should appear in moderation, if at all, in a short story.

For the purposes of this exercise, though, you should feel free to flip through a thesaurus as much as you want.

Below you will find five descriptions. Sometimes, they appear as complete sentences, sometimes as fragments. Your job this week is to say each another way. So, for instance, I might give you something like:

"They stared at each other a long time." (If I had a nickel for every time someone stared at someone else for a long time in my novel, I wouldn't be writing this book, as I'd be busy relaxing at my castle in the Mediterranean.)

Your job is to pretend that you're at the second point in your story or novel where someone is about to stare at someone else for a long time. You've already used "They stared at each other a long time." Your mission now is to come up with a new way to describe the same action. But that's not all! After you come up with a fresh description, you have to do it again—and again: A total of three times. (Because people are going to stare at each other a long time in your story more than once again.) What might your answers be? I give you one more than required below.

1. They looked and looked at each other.

2. They kept their eyes on one another for minutes.

3. Each considered the other as the clock ticked on the mantel.

4. A long silence passed, their eyes on each other.

Obviously, you don't have to change every word in the line; just change enough to make the sentence sound different. Help yourself by identifying every key element in the sentence—the staring, the staring *at one another*, the long time doing it—and render each in a fresh way. (If you find yourself wanting to add a new element, that's fine.)

Of course, the trick is to do so without making the sentence sound ridiculous—as my #2 does a little bit. (It reads like the characters are participating in a bug-out contest.)

Your assignment: Below are five descriptions. Please come up with three variations on each.

1. The sun rose.

2. … tapping on the table impatiently with his fingers.

3. The airplane blinked its way through the star-studded sky.

4. The assembled erupted in laughter.

5. Tossing the pebble into the water…

CHALLENGE EXERCISE:

Take five published books from the shelf, open each, close your eyes, and pick a spot with your finger. Re-write the sentence your finger landed on in three ways. If you happen to choose a not very substantial sentence, choose another one.

ADVERBS INTO DESCRIPTIONS OR ACTION VERBS

Purpose: To learn how to work adverbs into action verbs.

This week, let's start with a quick grammar refresher: What's an adverb? An adverb is a word that describes *how* an action is performed. (Adverbs often end in *-ly*.) If someone is taking her time to say something, she's speaking *slowly*. If she's thinking a lot about her words, she's speaking *carefully*. And so forth. Literature uses adverbs all the time. I just opened a novel at hand, Albert Camus' *The Stranger*, randomly to page 45, and had to read only about a dozen lines before arriving at: "'Take that cigarette out of your mouth when you're talking to me,' the policeman said *gruffly*."[5] [Italics mine.]

So, what's wrong with adverbs? If they're good enough for Albert Camus, a legendary writer, they're good enough for us, right? Yes and no. Imagine if Camus' line had said: "'Take that cigarette out of your mouth when you're talking to me,' the policeman *snarled*." You would take away the same things from the sentence, wouldn't you? The difference is that "gruffly" —an **adverb**—explains to you that the policeman is gruff. "Snarled" —an **action verb**, in that it's a **verb** (snarl) that describes an **action**—**shows** it to you, allowing you to conclude it for yourself. The difference is subtle but critical. With "snarled," the author gives the reader the tools and the reader builds an impression using them. It's a collaborative effort—the author invites the reader to participate

5 Camus, Albert. *The Stranger*, trans. Stuart Gilbert. (New York, NY: Vintage Books, 1954), p. 45.

in the moment. Over the course of a short story or a novel, this serves to involve the reader much more deeply in the story than a list of I'll-explain-it-to-you adverbs. Adverbs tend to leave the reader out in the cold; action verbs bring the reader in.

It would be very difficult, and silly, to write a story or novel without adverbs. But an excess of adverbs can make a novel less exciting because over time, it starts to feel like the author keeps telling us what we should feel about a given moment rather than allowing us to make up our minds for ourselves. Take our segment about two friends, Lily and Cassandra, from Week 1. The original appears below, followed by a Version B. Please read both, paying attention to what's different.

Original

"You want to stay long?" Lily asked, her face pale.

Cassandra peeled herself away from the tomatoes. "What's *with* you?"

"Nothing," Lily rushed to say. "I've never been here before, you know."

"You've never come to the garden your daddy keeps?" Cassandra said.

"So what?" Lily said.

Version B

"You want to stay long?" Lily asked fearfully.

Cassandra peeled herself away from the tomatoes. "What's with you?" she said condescendingly.

"Nothing," Lily said defensively. "I've never been here before, you know."

"You've never come to the garden your daddy keeps?" Cassandra said skeptically.

"So what?" Lily said roughly.

I made six changes in Version B. Can you list what they are? (Don't look at the answers below until you do your best.)

1. _____

2. _____

3. _____

4. _____

5. _____

6. _____

Here they are, in bold (I number the lines so we can discuss them later):

1. "You want to stay long?" Lily asked **fearfully**.

2. Cassandra peeled herself away from the tomatoes. "What's **with** you?"
3. **she said condescendingly.**

4. "Nothing," Lily said **defensively**. "I've never been here before, you know."

5. "You've never come to the garden your daddy keeps?" Cassandra said **skeptically**.

6. "So what?" Lily said **roughly**.

Let's discuss a couple:

1. In the first line, I changed "her face pale" to "fearfully." These indicators do the same work—they alert you that Lily is afraid. But "fearfully," the adverb, spells it out for you, whereas "her face pale" —a **description**—*shows* it to you. Lines 4, 5, and 6 work in a similar way.

2. Adverbs also make a story more wordy. Arguably, "What's with you" does everything necessary to clue in the reader that Cassandra is puzzled by her friend. To help things along, I italicized "with," so the reader hears an emphasis on that word.

"What's *with* you?" makes it pretty clear: Cassandra is puzzled, maybe even annoyed by her friend. "She said condescendingly" is both unnecessary and shuts out the reader in the way discussed in #1.

Descriptions like "her face pale" and **action verbs** like "snarled" do the same work—they show the reader what's going on. Sometimes, even *they* are unnecessary—a really good line of dialogue makes clear what's going on without any help, whether it's from action verbs, descriptions, or adverbs. But if you want to give the reader an extra nudge, you want to use those adverbs sparingly and lean on descriptions and action verbs instead.

Before you go on to this week's assignment, let's practice converting this segment, which features either dialogue-only or dialogue-with-descriptions, into dialogue with help from action verbs only.

So, the first line in this version could read:

"You want to stay long?" Lily **shivered**.

The second line might read:

"What's *with* you?" Cassandra **squinted**.

Notice the space-saving work performed by the action verb. Cassandra squinting—an indication she's perplexed, or annoyed—saves the author from having to "peel herself from the tomatoes," a description meant to indicate reluctance.

Can you re-write the next three lines so they feature action verbs instead? Your first step should be to look at the **dialogue tag**—for instance, in the next line, "rushed to say." Here, we already have an action verb, so the sentence can stay as is or you can try to think of another action verb, such as "shrugged." Let's look at the next sentence. No adverb here, only the verb "said." In most cases, this would be a fine choice—the plainest, least glitzy verb is often the best because you don't want the reader to think you're trying too hard. But for the purposes of this exercise, let's practice. What action verb could replace "said" here to indicate Cassandra's surprise and/or confusion?

Same goes for the third sentence.

"Nothing," Lily rushed to say. "I've never been here before, you know."

"You've never come to the garden your daddy keeps?" Cassandra said.

"So what?" Lily said.

We're working with dialogue here, but I should note that the adverbs-into-action-verbs-or-descriptions rule applies just as readily to narration. Here's Camus again: "So it was a relief when we closed down and I was strolling *slowly* along the wharves in the coolness."[6] (Italics mine.) Arguably, Camus doesn't need the adverb because he already has an action verb on his hands—"strolling." "Strolling" means "walking slowly." (I should point out here that I'm relying on a translation, as I don't speak French. Perhaps the original doesn't commit this "sin.")

Note as well that plenty of adverbs are both useful and guiltless. Take one last sentence from Camus' novel: "I took a flying jump, landed **safely**…"[7] As I mentioned before, the goal isn't to avoid all adverbs, only enough to involve the reader in the story in the way described above.

Now, on to **your assignment:** Below appear 10 sentences, five of them dialogue, five narration. Each one ends with an adverb. For each of the 10 sentences, do two things: Outfit it with a description that replaces the adverb; then outfit it with a more vivid action verb in place of the present bolded verb. I've done the first one for you so that you know what I'm looking for.

1. The principal stood **quickly**.
    The principal stood, his fingers twitching with exasperation.
    The principal leaped up.

2. "This is the last time I can give you this kind of warning," he said **sniffily.**

6 Ibid, p. 32.
7 Ibid, p. 31.

3. Malcolm looked at the older man **sneeringly**.

4. "I would like a reply," the principal said **sternly.**

5. "You didn't ask a question," Malcolm said **nastily**.

6. The principal sat down **heavily**.

7. "Malcolm, how long will this go on?" he said **wearily**.

8. "You're the boss," Malcolm said **indifferently**.

9. The principal looked out the window **distractedly**.

10. Malcolm looked at the ceiling **aimlessly**.

Note:

One sentence-improvement solution this exercise doesn't consider is the removal of the adverbs without replacing them with anything. Really good dialogue will make clear what's happening without the aid of descriptions or action verbs, and it's often hard to improve on the straightforward simplicity of "said," the most invisible of all the verbs, as I mentioned above. But once in a while your sentence will need a little bit more and that's what this exercise practices.

CHALLENGE EXERCISE:

Make this lesson unnecessary. Write a 10-sentence fragment of a story—five sentences of dialogue, five sentences of narration—that makes what's going on so clear that no descriptive aids are necessary—not adverbs, not action descriptions, not action verbs. In fact, no dialogue tag other than "said" should appear in the fragment.

FICTION • SECTION 3

DESCRIPTION

WEEKS 6 - 7

THE CHICKPEA EXERCISE

Purpose: To come up with imaginative comparisons.

We've just reminded ourselves of the value of vivid description. Now it's time to practice it. This week, we will take as our inspiration a short article that appeared in *The New Yorker* magazine on July 20, 2009. It featured a conversation with the actor Paul Giamatti, who had just appeared in a film called *Cold Souls*. In this comedy of sorts, a company called Soul Storage offers, to those troubled by their souls, a service known as soul extraction. Giamatti's character's soul turns out to look like a chickpea, which makes him quite upset. In *The New Yorker* article, the interviewer, Tad Friend, draws out the actor on what the souls of some famous people might look like. Here is Giamatti imagining the soul of the actor Al Pacino: "It's a liquid, an oily liquid that gets into cracks and crevices, but also has some body to it."

The country singer Merle Haggard: "An engine block. Powerful, but kind of rusty, with lots of buildup."

Former Guns N' Roses guitarist Slash: "A blood orange, left out on a windowsill, all dried out and leathery."

Former North Korean leader Kim Jong Il: "A crazy box of crabs."

Giamatti himself: "A hand-painted ceramic toad."[8]

---

8 Friend, Tad, The Pictures, "Soul Man," in *The New Yorker*, (July 20, 2009), p. 25.

Why am I bringing all of this up? Because in this article Paul Giamatti comes up with some wonderful descriptions. Asked to reduce each of these individuals to their essences, he comes up with vivid, memorable imagery. Even if you don't know who Merle Haggard is, you can imagine what kind of person he is, I bet, by reading a description like the one above.

This week, in order to flex our descriptive muscles, we're going to perform a similar feat.

Your job is to choose ten individuals—people you know, family members, celebrities, politicians, historical figures; you name it—and come up with a metaphorical image for each. The image can consist of a single-word—"rhinoceros" —or a longer description. ("Slow, winding, deliberate, like a rhino.") Do make sure that you use a single word for no more than five of the descriptions. Longer descriptions are better; it's more fun—and a better exercise—if you go on for a while describing the image, the way Paul Giamatti does above for Merle Haggard.

How to do this? Your first task is to try to pin down what quality of the person in question you would like to highlight. This forces you to spend some time thinking about the "essence" of the person. A tall friend (physical appearance) may make you think of a giraffe, but so might an inquisitive friend (character) who is always inclining his neck, so to speak, to find out what's going on. Try to think of genuine comparisons: "Chatterbox" is too literal a description for your younger brother. If his dominant quality is his talkativeness, you might come up with something like "a radio." Better yet, you might come up with:

"A radio that someone keeps on the whole day as they go about their house chores."

This is a far more imaginative solution—it conjures a whole scene rather than a single item. In Level Three of this series, I introduced the concept of the **authenticating detail.** It's the very specific detail in a story that makes you feel like you're really there. In this case, it's the part of the description that follows after "a radio." Can't you imagine yourself there?

A comparison also tries to evoke how something *feels* as much as what something looks or acts like. So you might ask yourself how a particular quality makes you feel. If your brother's endless chattering exhausts you, you might come up with a comparison like "a yawping spaniel" or "a thick textbook," rather than "chatterbox." Neither has to do with human talkativeness literally, but both suggest a kind of annoying exhaustion.

Your assignment: Come up with 10 individuals whose "souls," personalities, or characters you'd like to describe through comparisons. Then do it. Remember to push yourself beyond simple or literal comparisons. Let your mind wander.

CHALLENGE EXERCISE:

We're practicing these comparisons because they do *a lot* to spice up literature. Compare "Billy Sorenson, tired, fell into bed" and "Billy, a wrung towel, fell into bed." Which one is more vivid? So, in this challenge exercise, take the next step and come up with 10 characters and 10 metaphors to describe either their essential qualities or their conditions in that moment. Aim for complete sentences. A couple of examples follow:

"Ruth, a snail, covered her ears to shut out the storm."

"He sprung from his crouch, a pitchfork."

"Philip Dowell, a wrinkled briefcase of a man…"

INTERIORITY

Purpose: To practice writing from the inside of a character's mind.

What is interiority? It refers to our interiors—the stuff going on inside our minds, our hearts, even our bodies. In your reading and writing, you may have noticed that not all action takes place outside the characters' inner selves. Some of the action takes place inside characters' minds. The reader is invited along as the author has the character ruminate on something or other (let's call it **meditation**), or observe something (let's call it **perception**).

Readers tend to respond more easily to **action** than narration of what's going on in a character's mind. In the previous levels of this series, we've talked about suspense as important to reader interest. What kind of suspense is there in watching an accountant puzzle through the meaning of, say, a conversation he had with a co-worker? Or a fisherman go on about the colors and dents of the boat he's taking out for a day in the water? But getting inside a character's head is a critical part of understanding him well enough to make him feel lifelike to the reader. The challenge, then, is to figure out how to do so in order that the reader's attention doesn't wane.

This week, your assignment is to write 500 words entirely from a character's mind. No action can take place. You can describe a character thinking something through (meditation), or you can describe him observing something (perception). Below are brief examples of both.

THINKING THROUGH AN EXAMPLE:

1. "Where was he, where was he, where was he? He had gone off to school—she had put him on the bus herself. He had been to his classes—the school had confirmed that. But when the bus slid open its doors at the top of their drive, no one emerged. He wasn't the kind of boy to go off without permission. Without thinking of her, her worrying! He would have called. Right? He would have called. They had talked about this—you want to spend the afternoon at the Lewises, you *call* me. You *call* me. How could he be so thoughtless, how? Everything you said to him, it went through him like a sieve."

What did I do here? Let's go step-by-step. In the first instance, I had to come up, for starters, with a character, a situation, and something in that situation worth puzzling through. Let's say you have a mother whose child has gone missing (for this exercise, you don't need to figure out the plot beyond this). What might such a mother ruminate about for 500 words? You could jot down the possibilities before you get started: She might comb through the options of where her son has disappeared to; she might think about past times he'd gone off; she might think about the kind of boy he is—is he willful? obedient?; she might think about whether to alert the authorities.

Note, by the way, the tone of the segment. It's rushed and anxious. The sentences are mostly short and come tumbling one after the next. Others run on, full of commas and clauses. Some repeat themselves, the way a frantic mind will repeat something over and over, or go over the same details. This is **form** mimicking **content** once more. Because the mother is anxious, her thoughts read anxiously. The author is trying to re-create for the reader a little bit of what it's like to feel what the mother is feeling.

Did you notice, as well, some of the characteristics that make clear this is the interior working of someone's mind? The mother engages in a kind of dialogue with herself, asking questions and then answering them, and exclaiming to no one in particular.

Note also the shifting patterns of the woman's emotions. She starts out listing the facts, then tries to reassure herself by reminding herself this is a boy who wouldn't be so inconsiderate as not to call. But then this benefit of the doubt shifts to impatience and even anger: "How could he be so thoughtless, how? Everything you said to him, it went through him like a sieve."

So, here is a checklist of questions/steps you might set out for yourself as you start and work:

1. What's the character and what's the situation?

2. What might this character have to ruminate about, considering the situation?

3. Does the tone of the passage mimic the emotional condition of the character?

4. In what ways do I make clear this is someone's internal monologue?

5. How do the character's feelings shift throughout the passage?

You can answer and map out as many of these questions as you would like before starting. You may want to think about some of the methods authors use in plotting out their stories. I've discussed this in previous levels of this series, but here's a refresher: Some map out every little thing they're going to write, drawing an outline on a piece of paper. Some plan no further than the first sentence, or a very broad idea of what's going to happen. A third set—and this group includes me—fall somewhere in the middle: They plot out the major strokes of the story—in this case, I might map out how the character's mood shifts throughout the piece—and only then begin.

2. That's how a character thinking something through, the first option given to you, might work. For the second example—"observing something"—let's work in reverse, answering these questions before trying our hand at a segment. Question by question, here's an example:

1. What's the character and what's the situation?
A: Let's use the example, above, of a fisherman having a look over his boat before he takes it out for a day of fishing.

2. What might this character have to ruminate about, considering the situation?
A: What if the catch has been low, and the weather's turning, so there's not much fishing left in the season? This set-up could lead to any number of ruminations, but let's leave it at that during this planning stage.

3. Does the tone of the passage mimic the emotional condition of the character?

A: Usually, I don't plan out something of this detail in advance—I hope ideas will come to me as I'm writing—but for the purposes of this exercise, let's talk about it. How is our character feeling? Slow and mournful, I think, so I'm seeing leisurely, flowing sentences—never too short and declarative—going on clause after clause. This mimics the lapping of the water, too. (Note: Form doesn't *have to* mimic content. Also, it's likely to end up mimicking content no matter what. If you're working hard to imagine the state of mind of an individual in a slow, mournful mood, your prose is not going to pop with exclamation marks.)

4. In what ways do I make clear this is someone's internal monologue?
A: This one will have to wait till the writing itself.

5. How do the character's feelings shift throughout the passage?
A: The emotional arc of the passage can go in many directions. Our fisherman could start off slow and mournful; then turn angry at the low yield of the catch this season, and at the wholesalers who won't offer higher prices per pound; then settle into the recognition that this is his life and this is what he's going to do until the end of his days. Or all this can go in a very different direction—the fisherman might decide to sink his boat, so as to force himself to look for a different line of work. Or the slowness-and-mournfulness can turn to a kind of nobility, pride, and faith by the end of the passage.

Now, to the passage itself:

Here's what I might come up with, after answering the questions above.

> She was rusty, a bit, here and there, and on her hull, she carried the marks of 10 oceans. He hadn't wanted to give her a name—he hated the familiar way the other fishermen took with their boats; it was an occupation, not a friendship—but after a dozen years on the water, he knew her better than his own family. So did that mean he could give a dozen years to anything, and he'd be as expert as he was with her? But what kind of expert was he, if he couldn't even pay his costs?
>
> Why was it a she? He had no idea. If he ever went fishing for fun, it would be with a buddy, not some gal. But it felt right for the boat to be a lady. She had that grace. She had that patience. She was a 30-foot trawler, with

a long swooping prow that made him think of the old Cape Cod dories, though with a single-screw diesel. She was no kind of relic.

Note that this **observation** passage starts off with some **meditation** on the fisherman himself and the boat. There's no reason you can't combine the two; in fact, most "interiority" segments will.

Note, as well, the slight chauvinism of the words "not some gal," and then the very concept that this gentleman wouldn't go fishing with a woman. Is this particularly sensitive or enlightened? Perhaps not, but I'll remind you that, in fiction, your job isn't to be politically correct, or over-respectful. Fiction, obviously, isn't a place for prejudice, if only because prejudice tends to be one-sided, and that makes for boring writing. But your job, as author, is to present characters warts and all, and this fisherman's discomfort around women—it's more like shyness, actually—is part of who he is. (By the way, in the previous volume, we discussed **writing against type**: Just because we imagine most commercial fishermen as salty-dog types more comfortable sidled up to a bar than a kitchen sink, it doesn't have to be that way in a story. A commercial fisherman who changes diapers would be an exciting departure from the stereotype.)

Note also the research that has gone into this segment. I decided to write about a commercial fisherman down on his luck because the emotional drama of this appealed to me. But I don't know the first thing about fishing and boats! So I had to spend a little time online, looking up what the various parts of a fishing boat were called, and talking to a friend who has been sailing his whole life. (This is something else we covered earlier in the series—researching different kinds of lives and what people do in them.)

My final note is about point of view: Despite the fact that we are in these characters' minds, we are not being led through the story by them. We are being led by a third-person narrator who refers to the mother, in Example 1, as "she" and the fisherman, in Example 2, as "he." It's ironic, isn't it, considering that we're so deep inside these characters' minds? But that doesn't have to affect point of view. I decided on third-person narrators in these segments because it allowed me to be a fly on the wall, so to speak. I wanted to see what the characters were thinking and seeing, but I wanted to decide for myself what that meant, how it sounded, and so forth. Also, being in third-person allowed me to provide context for the reader that would have sounded silly coming from the character—who knows the information already—herself or himself.

Your assignment: Pick a character and write 500 words entirely from that character's mind. You can do as much (or as little) preparatory work (answering the questions above) as you find useful.

CHALLENGE EXERCISES:

1. If you produced a passage of meditation, produce one of perception, or vice versa.

2. Re-write your segment, using the first-person point of view.

PACING

TIME IN FICTION

Purpose: To practice rendering passage of time in a short story.

Let's read this paragraph from the short story "The Mourners" by Bernard Malamud.[9]

> Kessler, formerly an egg candler, lived alone on social security… He was much alone, as he had been most of his life. At one time he'd had a family, but unable to stand his wife or children, always in his way, he had after some years walked out on them. He never saw them thereafter, because he never sought them, and they did not seek him. Thirty years had passed. He had no idea where they were, nor did he think much about it.

I wanted to share this passage because of its remarkable handling of the passage of time. "Thirty years had passed." In a single sentence! But that's not all. Notice as well: "…he had **after some years** walked out on them." Those three little words—"after some years"—account for quite a few years!

A former professor in my graduate writing program used to refer to this kind of maneuver as "**the glide**." In just a handful of words—only 84, by my count—the author "glides" us across years and decades. Some authors can even "glide" us past centuries, if need be.

---

9 Malamud, Bernard. *The Magic Barrel.* (New York, NY: Vintage, 1962), p. 17

This week, we're going to practice "the glide" ourselves. We'll also practice its opposite: bringing so much attention to a brief moment, lasting mere seconds, that we'll have enough to say about it to fill 500 words. My old professor never shared a term for this kind of maneuver, so we'll have to coin something ourselves. Let's call it "**the toffee**." Sounds strange, but think about it: We're stretching a brief moment far beyond its actual length.

First things first: Why do we need "the glide"? The answer is in the passage above. Sometimes, in order to begin, a story needs some backstory—the reader needs some information about what happened before the start of the story in order to make sense of what's about to come. It would have been so laborious if the author, Bernard Malamud, first took us, using scenes, through Kessler's arguments with the wholesalers who used to employ him, and then his arguments with his family, and so forth. Instead, Malamud summarizes those events in Kessler's life and glides right into the present.

Same goes for "the toffee." Sometimes, an author will want to highlight some moment with so much emphasis that instead of saying "He rose," she'll choose to go on for 10 sentences about a character's standing up. More often than not, however, the author won't waste that kind of attention on something as simple as a character rising from a chair. (A character rising from his wheelchair for the first time? That's a different story.) She'll want to highlight something singular: A boxer's winning jab; a gorilla tracker laying her eyes on her first gorilla; the seconds before a bomb goes boom. Here, too, form mimics content: The seconds before a bomb goes boom probably feel like eternity, so describing them, and what might be going through a character's mind at length, is appropriate. (So do the seconds that follow after a dentist says, "I'm just going to drill for a second.") If Boxer A has been after Boxer B for years and is about to defeat him for the first time in his career, the lengthy chew-over of his winning maneuver corresponds to all the years he's waited for this moment. Same goes for the gorilla tracker—she's been after this sighting for years.

There are various ways to do the "toffee" part of this week's assignment. You could focus on an action of seconds that consists of so many mini-actions—a centipede moving its legs, a chemical reaction taking place—that you'll easily fill 500 words just by describing all the steps. That's clever, but not what I have in mind here. The idea is to focus so closely on an action that you notice all kinds of details that you would have otherwise skipped over. A boxer's winning jab is a single action—but there's the position of his feet in the ring, the feel of the sweat on his body, the noise coming from ringside, the facial expression of his opponent. And the jab itself is no single action—it's a coordination of his shoulders, his feet, and his waist. Surely, the boxer makes a noise as well as he delivers the jab. When you think closely, you'll notice enough things about the action to stretch it out into 1,000 words, not 500.

Here's my own stab at a "toffee" moment:

Oliver doesn't leap. Oliver soars. Oliver takes off like a spaceship you don't know will return. You know when it's about to happen because he gets a look in his eye. He's looking his blocker in the eyes, but his eyes go through the blocker, through the rest of the defense, up the alley, and into lay-up position. In his mind, Oliver has scored the deuce long ago. Now he just needs to execute it, to bring reality in line with his mind work. His shoulders swivel, his nostrils flare, and for a moment you expect fire. He takes a timid little step in the fake-out direction, so the blocker can think I've got him, I smell his blood.

And just when the blocker sets to pounce, well, then, you need slow-motion film. If your eyes aren't especially good, Oliver is a blur. Oliver is pirouetting like a ballerina. Oliver lunges like sumo. Oliver's shoulders are going toward Mars, and his legs toward Jupiter. He clears the boys in the defense like he's doing slalom. The boys stand still, or might as well. By the time they've turned toward him, they're breathing his exhaust. If you close your eyes you hear a ballet of squeaks on the well-oiled floor and an auditorium of 300 forgetting to breathe. But all this? All this is preview. Because now, the defense behind him, Oliver's set for the last part. Now he is ready. Now, Oliver soars.

The moment I describe above probably claims no more than a second or two on the court, but it easily lasts 250 words on the page. And, believe me, I could have gone on. Once you start noticing every little thing, you realize there are a million things to notice. I focused on narrating action, but I could have spent just as much time describing the sound of 300 people holding their breath, or the ticking clock, or the scoreboard, or the expressions on people's faces, or… or… or…

Your assignment: Write two segments. The first, "the glide," will resemble Bernard Malamud's at the start of this lesson. In 250 words, give me decades in the life of a man, woman, country, or what have you. If you want to cover centuries, be my guest. If you want to cover millennia, go for it.

In the second passage, you'll have to go on for 250 words about a moment lasting mere seconds. The exercise you did last week, where I asked you to have a character ruminate or observe, is a good example of how to fill 500 words with a moment probably lasting no more than seconds. Since you've already practiced that, try this week to lean on interiority as little as possible. Instead, describe what's actually going on with and around the character—that is, describe action.

CHALLENGE EXERCISE:

Re-read two favorite short stories, paying extra attention to how the passage of time is handled in each one. Work with a pencil. Make notes in the margins about how long the author takes to render particular moments, and whether he ever goes for "the glide" or "the toffee."

STRUCTURE AND TIMING

Purpose: To familiarize ourselves with basic notions of when to say what you want to say, and how much to say about it.

One of the most important, and elusive, skills in fiction is knowing how to organize the telling of a story. The author knows how things begin, and sometimes, how they end, but what's the right way to present the arc of the story to a reader?

One option is to tell it the way one tells a joke, or a story, at the family dinner table: From start to finish. This happened, then that happened, and this is how it turned out. This isn't a bad starting point. But drama is different from ordinary life—if a short story transcribed things exactly as they happened, the story would be quite long, and also quite boring. We don't notice it because we're living it, but life is full of dull, empty, and meaningless moments, silences, and stretches where nothing happens. More often than not, a story will leave those out.

Remember Oliver, our basketball player from last week? A story about something having to do with his basketball exploits might spend a whole paragraph closely observing his technique as he avoids defenders on his way to the basket, but it's unlikely to spend 10 pages itemizing every aspect of his practice routine. Just before the buzzer sounds, with Oliver's team one point down as he drives to the basket, the story might increase suspense—by taking a time-out to recall, briefly, Oliver's endless practice of the maneuver he's undertaking now on the court. We might see him trudging to the school gymnasium in the snow; shooting baskets into the early hours of the morning, the janitors locking up around him; we might even travel back to his days as a young boy and what basketball meant to him then.

But go on too long about this stuff—backstory—and the reader will start to get antsy. *Get me back to the court!* the reader itches. *I want to know what happens! Does Oliver make the basket? Does his team win?* So, a little backstory in the right moment can increase suspense by delaying the answer the reader is looking for—he starts reading more and more quickly in order to get back to the court, to find out how things end— and reading quickly is always what you want from your reader. But go on too long and the string of the story, growing ever more taut, snaps, and the reader gets annoyed. Above all, the fiction writer is a kind of acrobat, stretching that string as far as it will go before it snaps. The author must be a master calibrator of what to say, how much to dwell on it, and when to mention it.

This week, we'll spend a little time familiarizing ourselves with the basics of **structure** and **timing in fiction**. A lot of it you know already, if only instinctively. You've been writing scenes and summary, filling in backstory, and moving the story forward for weeks if not years. In this week's work, I just want to call attention to the tools you've been using, so that you can wield them with more knowledge and accuracy. So, let's explore a basic notion of structure and timing: What order should you put your scenes in? Where should you place the character's backstory? When should you reveal important information to the reader?

Here's the most important principle for you to remember: **Introduce your character through a scene, and only then give us his backstory.**

The first instinct of young writers is to introduce a character through backstory. They spend a couple of paragraphs explaining what kind of person Sam Robertson is. The idea is reasonable enough: How can I throw Sam into a scene if the reader can't make head or tail of him yet?

The trouble with this approach is that the reader doesn't yet care that much who Sam Robertson is. As the author drones on and on about, say, Sam's years in a factory, and then how Sam made his way out West, the reader struggles to care. He hasn't seen Sam *do* anything yet, so why should he pay attention to Sam's past?

Nothing invests a reader as deeply in a character as seeing that character speak, and act, as part of a scene. **Scene** brings a character alive far more than **summary**. (If that doesn't make immediate sense, think about a character in the last film you watched, and whether he would have seemed more or less alive if his actions in the story were described by a voice-over, the screen black, as opposed to what you saw.) So, an author might start his story with a scene of Sam at his modest kitchen table—one of its legs is about to come off and he's been duct-taping it back on since he moved in (remember **authenticating detail**?). It's the early hours of the morning, outside still dark, before he heads off to his job as an Oregon park ranger. We learn that Sam is fastidious—he washes all his dishes before he leaves—and that he is lonesome—his cereal grows soggy as he stares at someone's picture.

You'll agree that the above is hardly the height of drama, but it's enough to inform us that Sam is lonesome, that he's working a new job, that it has early hours, and so forth. We empathize with his loneliness; we wonder whose picture he's looking at; we respond with a little pity to the modesty of his circumstances. We have become connected to this man, and we are curious to find out what will happen during his day in the woods. What a sleight of hand! Just by sharing a couple of personal details in scene, the author has gotten us to wonder about what's going to happen on an ordinary day in the life of a park ranger who was of no interest to us until a moment ago!

Now imagine if the author presented the same information in backstory:

> Sam Robertson had been a factory worker out East for 20 years when one day he abandoned his post after lunch hour and never came back. Trying to drive all thought out of his mind for fear it would make him realize what a mistake he was making and turn back, he packed a quick bag, folded himself into his ancient Mazda, and set out West, pictures of which he had been studying since he was a boy. He had never been, not once. He didn't know what awaited him there—but who does, he tried to reassure himself—and he had only one requirement for whatever work he found there: It had to take place outside. He wouldn't spend another day gathering grime on his hands on the factory floor, filing the same bolt over and over. Unlike a factory floor, nature, Sam Robertson said to himself as he crossed the Rockies and his mood lifted, was variable.

Now, this isn't a bad beginning. But if the previous version made me feel like I was in a room with Sam Robertson, observing him, in this version I feel like I'm sitting in an auditorium and watching Sam Robertson up on a screen. He's further away.

Note as well that I'm nearly 200 words into the story, and I haven't yet begun to complete the story of Sam's arrival in Beaverton, Oregon. If I've started down this road of providing backstory, I'll want to finish it, and it'll be paragraphs upon paragraphs before I say enough about it to start a scene of Sam on the morning in question (the cereal, the picture, etc.). By that point, chances are, the reader will be getting itchy for less summary and more scene. Had I started with a scene, had I gotten the reader into that room with Sam from the get-go, I would have earned quite a bit of patience for a backstory to follow the scene.

Make no mistake: There are masterful stories that begin with backstory. Take our opening example from last week, about Kessler, the egg candler. The author, Bernard Malamud, gives us a paragraph of backstory, but no more. He rushes to scene as quickly as he can. (Perhaps that's why he "glides" as far as he does—30 years in a sentence.)

Beginning writers often squirm at opening with scene because they wonder how the reader will grasp Sam in all his depth if the author hasn't gotten a chance to explain who this person is, and where he comes from, and why the reader should care. But readers are a lot more willing to observe a character in action without full background on his personality than sit through reams of backstory without having met the character "live," so to speak.

Also, this isn't an either-or game. My scene opening about Sam Robertson can include a tactical sentence here and there clarifying what's happening in the scene through a quick bit of backstory. But here's where that instinct for calibration has to come into play—a reader will tolerate a sentence of backstory, maybe two, but then, let's get back to the scene, please.

This week, you'll practice starting a story with a scene, then following up with a character's backstory, for 500 words. (Aim for 250 words of scene, followed by 250 words of backstory.) Feel free to seed a sentence or two of backstory in the opening scene to clarify things, but in that opener, the focus should be on presenting the character in some kind of environment. Note, by the way, that scene here doesn't mean that a character has to be speaking to someone else, though that's fine, too. We simply need to be in the same room with him or her. In fact, let that be your barometer—does the scene read as if we're in the room with the character? If you aren't sure, ask your mentor to weigh in.

Let's review your steps. You're going to start this story the way you do so many others—by coming up with a character in a situation. Your next step might be to map out the character's backstory, to the extent it's relevant for the story—who is he or she? Where did he or she come from? Why is he or she doing what he or she's doing? What will happen, in broad terms, throughout the story? These are the notes from which you'll conjure a scene to open the short story (*you* need the backstory early, but the reader does not). Before diving into the scene, you might jot down a couple of possibilities for how and where we might observe the character in action. What follows after is gravy—250 words of backstory, which you already have because you started out by brainstorming about it.

Before I send you off, here's an example from my own writing. As you read, try to step outside yourself and observe your feelings in response to the character in question. In this segment, I start with a scene, followed by backstory. As an experiment, I run the segment a second time but with the tables turned—backstory first, scene second. Think about which version interests you more—and when—in the characters, and why.

The below is a conversation between an elderly man ("Grandfather") whose wife has just passed away and another man ("Rudolf Kozlovich," "Rudik") who owns most of the burial plots in the cemetery where Grandfather wants to bury his wife. Slava is Grandfather's grandson.

VERSION 1: SCENE FIRST, BACKSTORY SECOND

"Yevgeny Kharitonovich," a man called out. Grandfather looked up and nodded ponderously. His eyes went searching the room. Somehow, Slava knew they were searching for him. When they found him, Grandfather tweaked his eyebrows. When Slava approached, Grandfather extended his arm, and Slava took it.

"My condolences, from the bottom," the man said to Grandfather, covering his heart with his palm. He was six feet tall, in a leather jacket, his lined bricklayer's face crowned by a short ponytail. A tiny gold hoop roosted in one of the ears. He reached out a grate of hairy knuckles and collected Grandfather's limp palm.

"Thank you, Rudik, thanks," Grandfather said.

"Are you looking?" the man said.

"Yes, yes," Grandfather said. "We need."

"Step into the office?"

"This is my grandson," Grandfather said, turning to Slava.

"Rudolf Kozlovich," the man extended his hand. "What do you—"

"He's studying, still," Grandfather said.

In the office, Kozlovich unfurled a bluish map of Washington Cemetery.
It was a small city with avenues and streets named after trees—Walnut,
Maple, Ash. McDonald Avenue ran through the middle, the train
thundering above.

"Nothing by the fence," Grandfather said.

"They've got Astroturf on it now," Kozlovich said. "That green stuff they put
on the soccer field. You can't see in."

"Nothing by the fence," Grandfather repeated.

Kozlovich's finger traced a line to the other half of the grounds. "The head
office is on this side."

"That means what?"

"The grounds crew checks in there. More people around. Downside is—not
too far from the train, either."

"Where is the quietest?"

"Quiet's over here." Kozlovich slid his finger across hundreds of graves. "They're building new condominiums on that side, but that's practically over. Tulip Lane."

"She loved tulips," Grandfather said.

"Meant to be, then," Kozlovich opened his hands.

Rudolf Kozlovich was known. He had come from Odessa in 1977 or 1978. He had a look around and settled on a plan. One day, he and some hired boys hijacked a truck of Macy's furs. Sable, mink, fox. Then they returned them one by one at the branch stores, just a lot of husbands coming back with unsuccessful gifts. They were done, more than a hundred thousand dollars between them, before the store could piece together what had happened. With his one hundred thousand, Rudolf purchased one hundred choice plots at the cemetery on Bay Parkway and McDonald Avenue.

There he was at the hospital, at the funeral home. He had an information network—oncologists, nurses, funeral-home directors—that Macy's security could only envy. Kozlovich's business was unofficial, of course, spread between different owners who collected small percentages for the use of their names in the contracts, and the cemetery continued to own some of the plots. But Kozlovich's were the rarest, and, as fewer of them remained, the prices went up.

"I want two," Grandfather said.

"Yevgeny Kharitonovich," Kozlovich's forehead rose. "A plot in advance? You're tempting fate."

VERSION 2: BACKSTORY FIRST

"Yevgeny Kharitonovich," a man called out. Grandfather looked up and nodded ponderously. His eyes went searching the room. Somehow, Slava knew they were searching for him. When they found him, Grandfather tweaked his eyebrows. When Slava approached, Grandfather extended his arm, and Slava took it.

Rudolf Kozlovich was known. He had come from Odessa in 1977 or 1978. He had a look around and settled on a plan. One day, he and some hired boys hijacked a truck of Macy's furs. Sable, mink, fox. Then they returned them one by one at the branch stores, just a lot of husbands coming back with unsuccessful gifts. They were done, more than a hundred thousand dollars between them, before the store could piece together what had happened. With his one hundred thousand, Rudolf purchased one hundred choice plots at the cemetery on Bay Parkway and McDonald Avenue.

There he was at the hospital, at the funeral home. He had an information network—oncologists, nurses, funeral-home directors—that Macy's security could only envy. Kozlovich's business was unofficial, of course, spread between different owners who collected small percentages for the use of their names in the contracts, and the cemetery continued to own some of the plots. But Kozlovich's were the rarest, and, as fewer of them remained, the prices went up.

"My condolences, from the bottom," the man said to Grandfather, covering his heart with his palm. He was six feet tall, in a leather jacket, his lined bricklayer's face crowned by a short ponytail. A tiny gold hoop roosted in one of the ears. He reached out a grate of hairy knuckles and collected Grandfather's limp palm.

"Thank you, Rudik, thanks," Grandfather said.

"Are you looking?" the man said.

"Yes, yes," Grandfather said. "We need."

"Step into the office?"

"This is my grandson," Grandfather said, turning to Slava.

"Rudolf Kozlovich," the man extended his hand. "What do you—"

"He's studying, still," Grandfather said.

In the office, Kozlovich unfurled a bluish map of Washington Cemetery. It was a small city with avenues and streets named after trees—Walnut, Maple, Ash. McDonald Avenue ran through the middle, the train thundering above.

"Nothing by the fence," Grandfather said.

"They've got Astroturf on it now," Kozlovich said. "That green stuff they put on the soccer field. You can't see in."

"Nothing by the fence," Grandfather repeated.

Kozlovich's finger traced a line to the other half of the grounds. "The head office is on this side."

"That means what?"

"The grounds crew checks in there. More people around. Downside is—not too far from the train, either."

"Where is the quietest?"

"Quiet's over here." Kozlovich slid his finger across hundreds of graves. "They're building new condominiums on that side, but that's practically over. Tulip Lane."

"She loved tulips," Grandfather said.

"Meant to be, then," Kozlovich opened his hands.

"I want two," Grandfather said.

"Yevgeny Kharitonovich," Kozlovich's forehead rose. "A plot in advance? You're tempting fate."

Finally, your turn.

Your assignment: Write 500 words presenting a character in a situation. The first 250 (or so) should be all scene; the next 250, backstory.

CHALLENGE EXERCISE:

Re-write your segment so that backstory comes first, as it must in some stories. Use Bernard Malamud as your guide and barometer. Limit yourself to a backstory paragraph of no longer than 84 words.

FICTION • SECTION 5

VOICE/STYLE

EXAMINING LITERATURE FOR STYLE

Purpose: To recognize and practice voice and style in literature.

Have you ever heard someone talking about a book's "voice"? Books don't have voices, do they? Not literally, of course, but books do have personalities. A comedy might have a mood of hilarity and hijinks; a drama might be more solemn and emotional. But voice goes beyond this. What one author describes one way another author will describe completely differently. One author likes spare prose ("He stood"), another more elaborate styling ("He rose heavily from the chair, its legs scraping the parquet.") One likes shorter sentences, another longer. One likes black humor, another earnestness. One uses dialects, the other does not. The distinctions are a million.

Voice is one of the last things a writer develops—or, I should say, discovers. Each writer has his own, but when we start writing, either we can't help mimicking the writing we've seen, or we don't quite know what we're doing yet, so everything comes out sounding strained or awkward. You might have heard that mastery of a skill—violin, quarterbacking, backflips on a balance beam—takes 10,000 hours of practice. Finding your own true, authentic voice takes just about as long. It's something a writer discovers through endless practice and stumbling, and also lots and lots of reading.

We'll practice writing in different voices next week, but let's prepare ourselves this week by examining the styles of 10 writers. When we read, we tend not to stop to think about the *feel* of the narration—is it histrionic? grave? ironic? —because we're too busy trying to comprehend what's going on. So that's what we'll do this week. We'll look really closely at 10 sentences by 10 authors and try to find words for what they make us feel, in addition to making simple observations about aspects of style such as sentence length, tone, and so forth.

Below are the 10 sentences. Before you do anything else, read each of the sentences out loud. You'll notice that I've provided you with paragraph-long impressions about the voice used in five of them (3, 4, 7, 8, and 9). Read those paragraphs carefully.

(By the way, do you know what "histrionic" means? If not, did you stop and look it up?)

1. Ernest Hemingway: "The hills across the valley of the Ebro were long and white."[10]

2. Vladimir Nabokov: "It surprised him to realize how fond he had been of his teeth. His tongue, a fat sleek seal, used to flop and slide so happily among the familiar rocks, checking the contours of a battered but still secure kingdom, plunging from cave to cove, climbing this jag, nuzzling that notch…"[11]

3. Bernard Malamud: "[The tea] tasted bitter and he blamed existence."[12]

> Malamud's line reminds me of Hemingway's—as clear and sharp as a brisk morning, or a knife to the throat. After reading the first clause—"[The tea] tasted bitter" —I expected anything, anything at all—"so I added a lump of sugar," or "and I spilled it into the sink" —but the grand, startling sweep of "and he blamed existence." This characterizes much of Malamud's writing. Reading him, you get the sensation that he's gone over his words a hundred times, adding one in, taking one out, changing a third, until the sentence is as polished as a stone, and as lean as can be. But at the same time that he pares down the words, he enlarges their implication: This sentence, of just a handful of words, is a commentary on life itself, or at least one man's. So, to me, his prose feels at once chiseled and epic.

4. Nicholson Baker: "So I meant to go on to say this about repetition, treating it slightly more fully than I have been able to in renouncing my intention to treat it, but

---

10 Hemingway, Ernest. "Hills Like White Elephants," in *The Short Stories of Ernest Hemingway.* (New York, NY: Scribner, 1966), p. 273.
11 Nabokov, Vladimir. *Pnin.* (New York, NY: A. A. Knopf, 2004), p. 26.
12 Malamud, Bernard. *The Fixer.* (New York, NY: Farrar, Straus and Giroux, 2004), p. 5.

that word 'sky' has unexpectedly stopped the forward flow of my essay: not exactly with the lethal bottomlessness of the simple concrete word, but with that general more hypertrophied word..."[13]

> Can you understand what Baker is saying? (This, by the way, is the only nonfiction entry in this group of 10; *U and I* is a memoir of Baker's fascination with the novelist John Updike. *U and I*—get it?) I couldn't, and decided to spare you the rest of his sentence, which goes on and on, as many of Baker's sentences in this book tend to. I'd say Baker is too smart for his own good. The prose feels over-cerebral, turgid even. Endless clauses, one folding in on the next, $64 words like "hypertrophied," and all other kinds of bells and whistles. Perhaps we shouldn't take this as Nicholson Baker's voice, but as the voice of an admiring fan, frantic with excitement, tripping over his words, and blabbering on to no end. That would make it more tolerable.

5. Willa Cather: "The sun was still good for an hour of supreme splendour, and across the shining folds of country the low profile of the city barely fretted the skyline—indistinct except for the dome of St. Peter's, bluish grey like the flattened top of a great balloon, just a flash of copper light on its soft metallic surface.[14]

6. Herman Melville: "There are some strange summer mornings in the country, when he who is but a sojourner from the city shall early walk forth into the fields, and be wonder-smitten with the trance-like aspect of the green and golden world."[15]

7. Katherine Mansfield:

> "Shrugging his shoulders, the porter turned to me: 'Where for?' he asked.
> 'Ostend.'
> 'Wot are you putting it in here for?'
> I said, 'Because I've a long time to wait.'
> He shouted, 'Train's in 2.20. No good bringing it here. Hi, you there, lump it off!'[16]

13 Baker, Nicholson. *U and I: A True Story*. (London, UK: Granta, 1991), p. 87.
14 Cather, Willa. *Death Comes for the Archbishop*. (New York, NY: Vintage Books, 1990), p.3.
15 Melville, Herman. *Pierre or, the Ambiguities*. (New York, NY: Signet, 1964), p. 23.
16 Mansfield, Katherine. "The Journey to Bruges," in *The Short Stories of Katherine Mansfield*. (New York, NY: A. A. Knopf, 1937), p. 13.

This is the only dialogue entry in this group. I didn't include much dialogue because in dialogue, the characters' voices come through more than the author's, perhaps—though of course, the characters' voices are the author's as well—but this was such a distinctive piece of dialogue (dialect, I should say), that I wondered if we could find words for the feelings it inspires. I've purposefully left out context other than that we have here a porter and a train. So, what do we take away from this dialogue? It certainly draws attention to itself, through misspelling meant to mimic pronunciation ("Wot"), and the porter's sudden address of whoever "you, there" is instead of the narrator to whom he's just been speaking. Mansfield's story was written in 1910, so "lump it off" —lump a suitcase together with others—isn't a throwback by a modern writer; it was just the way people spoke then. But reading it in 2013 creates a powerful sense of being in another time. So, the voice here seems very grounded, and in the thick of things. It's not the voice of some remote, all-seeing author, but someone scrapping on the ground among the characters.

8. John le Carré: "In six years of honest labour in the world of commerce I have applied my services—be it by way of cautiously phrased conference calls or discreet meetings in neutral cities on the European continent—to the creative adjustment of oil, gold, diamond, mineral and other commodity prices..."[17]

None of the words above are "fancy," but there's a stiff formality to the way this gentleman expresses himself. After all, the sentence could be expressed much more simply. So I'm feeling like I'm in the hands of a real dandy who's going to regale me with great stories, but never unbutton his collar.

9. Alice Sebold: "The following morning Ruth was up early. Like Lindsey, Ruth was a floater at gifted camp. She didn't belong to any one group. She had gone on a nature walk and collected plants and flowers she needed help naming."[18]

17 le Carré, John. *The Mission Song*. (New York, NY: Little, Brown and Co., 2006), pp. 1-2.
18 Sebold, Alice. *The Lovely Bones*. (Boston, MA: Little, Brown, 2002), p. 115.

This quote feels like the palest of all the ones I've included here and demonstrates to me a critical difference between "plain" writing and "spare" writing. Hemingway is spare. Malamud is spare. There's that hard, polished gleam to their sentences. The hills are long and white—a description so pared-down as to seem generic, except it brings those hills alive in an almost mythical way. Both what Hemingway chooses to describe and how he describes it sounds to me like he rejected 50 versions of that sentence before settling on the one that appears in print. There's a difference between that kind of simplicity—it's a seeming effortlessness that reads so smoothly only after lots of trying—and the simplicity of describing something in the most obvious way. The latter describes the feel of Alice Sebold's sentence to me. It's elegant enough—it's not particularly verbose, and none of the words are clunky or especially generic. But if you or I were asked to express the thoughts Sebold expresses, we'd probably express them more or less as she does. The writing feels plainly informational rather than filled with style.

10. Nadine Gordimer: "It was in that first ambassadorial residence, behind gates where black guards strait-jacketed in gabardine and braid slouched on homemade stools, and sometimes a visiting wife and children squatted humbly behind the hibiscus, that she must have picked up, just as Marie-Claude had picked up, much that has made her assurance so provocatively perfect."[19]

Your assignment: Write a paragraph of your own impressions for each of the other five sentences (1, 2, 5, 6, and 10). How would you describe the tone, the feel, the voice? Use my analyses as a guide.

Here are some guideline questions to get you started, but try to use them as a departure point for your rumination on the style rather than an end in themselves. Writers practice so many styles that it's impossible to break them down according to an either-or set of questions.

1. Is the writing plain or rich?
2. Is there technical language?

19 Gordimer, Nadine. *A Sport of Nature.* (New York, NY: A. A. Knopf, 1987), p. 159.

3. Are the sentences long or short?

4. How would you describe the narrator—or whoever's speaking—in three adjectives?

5. What does the segment make you think of? Don't feel obligated to be literal; I am most curious what the segment makes you think of *outside* the story or novel.

CHALLENGE EXERCISE:

1. Draw connections and contradictions between the 10 sentences above. Who's spare, who's wordy? Who's sneering, who's earnest? Pay special attention to styles that share something—for example, the spareness in Hemingway and Alice Sebold—but not something else. (Sebold's prose, while "clear," feels a little simple. She expresses her point the way anyone would, more or less. Hemingway, while "clear" as well, has a kind of hard gleam that comes from working and re-working the sentence until it sounds like a particular individual—the narrator of his story—has uttered it, rather than some anonymous entity who could be anyone.)

2. Pick the five sentences above that you like the most. Then go to the library and read those works—if it's a short story; read the first 15 pages if it's a novel—by those authors, paying special attention to the style. Allow yourself to worry less about what the story "means" and focus instead on *how* it's being written.

THE SAME SITUATION IN A DIFFERENT VOICE

Purpose: To practice different styles of writing.

Now that we've learned a bit about the writing styles of published authors, let's try on some styles of our own. One way to do that is to write "in the style" of some author—either one from the list above or someone you love and whose style you know. Typically, this kind of copycatting has limited use. Inevitably, the author's style gets mixed with your own, whatever it is, and the resulting hybrid is neither his/her voice nor your own, but something stranded in between, and awkwardly so. (One thing that *is* useful, I've found, is to re-type sentences written by authors you love, as if they were your own. This comes closer to getting a feeling for what it might be like to be that writer, setting down those particular words in that particular way.)

We'll do something else this week. Below you'll find a paragraph of fiction, written as plainly as possible. Your job will be to re-write it, employing a different style. You can pretty up the prose through imaginative description; complicate the sentences by transforming the short, staccato ones below into long, flowing ones full of clauses; you can decide to use technical language; the options are many. The important thing is that you try to explore the possibilities of different writing voices.

After the paragraph below, I take a stab at a re-write of my own, followed by an analysis, as in the previous week, of what kind of voice I decided to try to inhabit. Read the example and my re-write and analysis before you go on.

PARAGRAPH:

The day dawned. There was mist on the lake. It curled above the surface of the water. The sun rose soon after. Loons made their calls. From the porch, Jennie cast a stone at the water. After its first bounce, it disappeared into the fog. Little by little, the day was warming and the fog was lifting. She took the porch steps to the bank of the lake and untied a canoe. It was old, dented, and had been painted several times. The nose of the canoe cut into the water. It glided over the calm surface of the lake. She entered the last wisps of fog. By the time she reached the other shore, she could see clearly behind her the cabin she had left. She tied up the canoe, looked around, and pulled a map from her pocket. Then she started to look for the body.

RE-WRITE:

The day dawned behind a wall of mist. It guarded the lake like a nervous mother, unwilling to let go, wisps of fog turning with menace over the water. A loon hooted from somewhere in the murk. From the porch, Jennie wondered if the loon was frightened inside that shroud of fog. What did a loon see? Had it seen what she had done? The murk had been just as thick that night. That's why Jennie had chosen it.

The sun rose higher. Jennie cast a stone at the silver glass of the lake, but instead of shattering, it swallowed the stone. Now, it was warmer. The fog counted its last moments, the sunlight awaiting its turn. Jennie took the porch steps to the wet grass and down to the bank, where her old canoe—dented; once-silver, now forest-green—bobbed in lapping water. She watched its nose slice into the frigid water of the lake with the satisfaction of an arrow.

The canoe streaked the flat water of the lake, the last wisps of fog dissipating around her. Nearing the bank, Jennie spun around. In the rising light of the sun, her cabin was clear on the other shore. The canoe poked the bank, Jennie dismounted, and tethered it to an old oak. Then the map came out. Then the search for the body began.

ANALYSIS:

Did you like the re-write? To be honest, I didn't, particularly. The moment—the cold morning, a young woman in a sober mood, a crime or accident—seems to call for less rather than more. My re-write tries for all kinds of fanciness—describing the fog as a nervous mother, for instance—and ascribes human qualities to the sunlight ("awaiting its turn") and the canoe, slicing through the water with "satisfaction." All this feels way too ornate for this moment.

In fact, while most of the sentences in the original version felt a little too clipped and, as a result, unnatural (this is also due to the fact that most of them are of a similar length, creating a feeling of monotony), I really liked the line "The nose of the canoe cut into the water." Describing the canoe's bow (front) as a nose *is* a metaphor, but it doesn't seem as far-fetched as "nervous mother" for the fog—the front of a canoe kind of looks like a nose, doesn't it? I liked the verb "cut" (or "sliced") here—the lakewater is as clear and still as glass. I also liked the rhythm of the words. All the words are short, never more than two syllables, and somehow that felt of a piece with the moment—a moment of few, spare, quick words.

The aim of this re-write exercise isn't necessarily to "improve" on the original, though of course there's plenty of room for improvement. It's to do something different, discovering through experiment and close attention all the decisions that go into style. The simple act of re-writing the same paragraph in different words is by definition an exercise in style because it gives you a taste of how many ways there are to say the same thing.

Your assignment: Re-write the paragraph yourself in a distinctive voice. It should be at least as long as the "plain" version, and might be significantly longer. You might find it useful to ask yourself the questions from Week 10 before you get started:

1. Will your writing be plain or rich?

2. Will there be technical language?

3. Will your sentences be long or short?

4. Who is the narrator? What three adjectives would you use to describe the narrator?

5. What do you want the reader to think about as he's reading your re-written paragraph?

CHALLENGE EXERCISES:

1. Write and re-write a paragraph of your own making. Aim for 150-250 words for each.

2. Pick one of the five authors whose stories/opening 15 pages you read last week. Then take his or her sample sentence from last week and extend it into a paragraph, mimicking that author's style. (You'll remember the general gist of the story/novel, but not the exact words.)

3. Do the same thing, but for an author you didn't read at length last week.

4. Pick your favorite author from last week, borrow the book in question from the library, and type/write out the first two pages of the story/novel in your own hand.

FICTION • SECTION 6

GENRE

FANTASY

Purpose: To acquaint ourselves with some of the basics of genre.

Genre is like voice—you know quite a bit about it already. What we're going to do this week is make some of that knowledge more explicit.

What is **genre**? For our purposes this week, we'll define it this way: Genre refers to different kinds of writing style. The writing we've been focusing on since the beginning of this year would most rightly be called **realist drama**—characters involved in experiences, often conflicts, that arouse the emotions. Those experiences happen in the real world—the one we live in now.

But there are many other literary genres: Epic, fable, fantasy, horror, crime, and many others. Each one has its own **conventions**, meaning stylistic criteria—prominent features that distinguish it from other kinds of genres. They have different tone, content, length, kinds of setting, types of characters...

For instance, fantasy fiction usually deals with otherworldly settings or characters, and asks the reader to suspend an understanding of reality as he or she knows it. Fantasy might feature magic, the supernatural, or imaginary worlds. Think of J. R. R. Tolkien's *The Lord of the Rings*, or C. S. Lewis' *The Chronicles of Narnia*, or L. Frank Baum's *The Wizard of Oz*. In fantasy, animals might speak, the earth might change shape, and the humans may be unable to see. The sky is the limit—if the story even has a sky.

Whether you're interested in fantasy or not—for instance, it's not my favorite literary genre—it is great practice to try your hand at it. When you write fantasy, you have to depart from the things you know. You may never again write a fantasy short story in your life. But by experimenting with it, you'll inevitably learn something about the genres that you *are* interested in.

Your assignment this week will consist of two parts. Read all the way through the steps before you get started.

First, I'll ask you to acquaint yourself with fantasy fiction more closely by reading a handful of—say, three—famous fantasy fiction works in the library.

These are mostly novels, so feel free to take just a glimpse—say, read the first five chapters or about 30 pages—before going on with the assignment. (Although, if you're hooked you should keep on reading!)

1. J. R. R. Tolkien, *The Hobbit* (and the three volumes of *The Lord of the Rings*)
2. Robert Jordan, *The Wheel of Time*
3. Ursula Le Guin, *A Wizard of Earthsea*
4. Stephen R. Donaldson, *Lord Foul's Bane*
5. Jonathan Stroud, *The Amulet of Samarkand*
6. Tad Williams, *The Dragonbone Chair*
7. Guy Gavriel Kay, *Tigana*
8. Richard Adams, *Watership Down*
9. Marion Zimmer Bradley, *The Mists of Avalon*
10. Terry Pratchett, *The Colour of Magic*[20]

As you read, try to notice the ways in which a fantasy story differs from ordinary drama. They should be pretty obvious—in our world, no piece of jewelry would ever have the extraordinary powers of the Ring in *The Lord of the Rings*—but make a point of noticing them anyway. You might guide yourself with some of our trusty 5 Essentials, modified for this exercise:

1. What is the plot of the story? Could this take place in a "realistic" story?
2. Who are the characters? Could they appear in a "realistic" story?
3. Where does the story take place? Could this be a "realistic" setting?

---

20 You can find many more recommendations at the Top 25 Best Fantasy Books website (http://bestfantasyb-ooks.com/fantasy-books.php).

4. What is the tone of the story? You'll notice that many fantasy stories take a tone that might remind you of fairy tale, or perhaps some of the epics you've read in your literary studies. Fantasy stories often borrow from folklore and mythology, and as a result, have a feel that might be described as magical. For extra credit, you might try to find words to describe that feel, which isn't easy.

The second part of your assignment this week will be to craft a story idea, plot, characters, and setting for a fantasy short story, largely as you did in Week 1, and then write 500 words from that story, whether from the beginning or some later scene.

Where to begin? I think the best way to start is to ask yourself whether you've ever had any interest in something around you working differently from the way it works. For instance, I love to travel. But traveling is a complicated endeavor—you need money, you need time to plan, you need time to familiarize yourself with your new surroundings. Usually, it feels all worth it in the end, but it's a lot of work! Also, sometimes I'll be reading a book about, say, Spain, and the author will be describing all kinds of very romantic things about the food, the culture, and the customs, and I'll think, "Oh, to be there now!" But the feeling often passes after I close the book. What if we could go anywhere we want for as briefly as we'd like, even five minutes?

So, if I was writing a fantasy story, I would build my story around this idea. But that's not enough, because even though fantasy stories deal with such different subject matter and tone, the conventions of storytelling still apply. (As the great writing teacher John Gardner puts it, "Dragons, like bankers and candy-store owners, must have firm and predictable characters.")[21] You still have to develop believable characters and interest the reader in turning the page. So my next step would be to imagine a character involved in some kind of extraordinary situation or conflict based on this premise. What if the narrator encounters some kind of charlatan who says he can bestow this gift on the narrator, but the narrator has to agree never to go anywhere, physically, ever again? Or, better yet, what if the narrator gets stuck in Spain long after he wants to come home? Or what if his body remains at home, but his mind is in Spain? The possibilities are many. This is exciting but also challenging: In creating fantasy, you often set yourself the task of changing the way *everything* works.

Your assignment:

Part One: Read the beginnings of three fantasy works. Notice the ways in which they are different from ordinary drama. Think about the 5 Essentials.

Part Two: Your turn. Come up with a plot, characters, and setting for a fantasy short story and compose 500 words of a scene, either from the beginning or somewhere later.

Part Two, modified: Changing *everything* about our world is hard work. If you're struggling, consider a modified version of this assignment: Change *one* thing, not *everything*.

Stay with me as I explain. Remember *Cold Souls*, the film I mentioned in Week 6? It's the story of a man who decides to have his soul extracted so it stops bothering him. This is a fantasy element—obviously, souls can't be extracted! —but everything else in the universe of the film is identical to life as we know it. There are no talking horses, no elves walking down the street, no magical concoctions.

In their reviews of the film, several critics picked up on the wisdom of this creative choice. Here's Manohla Dargis of *The New York Times*:

---

21 Gardner, John. *The Art of Fiction: Notes on Craft for Young Writers*. (New York, NY: Vintage Books, 1985), p. 21.

"It's a preposterous hook, of course, but Ms. Barthes introduces her absurd premise with deadpan restraint… There's a subset involving a world just like the one we inhabit, with only one element changed."[22]

And Anthony Lane of The *New Yorker*:

"To take a big, bewildering concept and treat it as a small, scuffed item of everyday use demands the kind of wit—literate and levelling—with which recent movies have all but dispensed… If you hark back to a fabulist like Buñuel, his wildest inventions were all the more coruscating for being filmed with a tranquil eye."[23]

Note: Do you know what "coruscating" means? Who Buñuel was? As always, if you stumble onto words or names or concepts you don't know, please look them up.

What the film critics are saying is that if the director, Sophie Barthes, made *every* element of her universe fantastical, it would a) drown out the uniqueness of the soul-extraction conceit, and, more importantly, b) it would make it less startling, less scary, because somewhere in our minds, we would register this alien universe as just that: alien. But if it's a world that looks exactly like ours, with just "one element changed," that's far more affecting, frightening even, because it makes us think: This could actually happen!

Just as important: Sophie Barthes presents this absolutely wacky concept as no big deal. No one in the film remarks on how wild, or crazy, it is that nowadays you can get your soul extracted. Soul-extraction is treated, indeed, as "a small, scuffed item of everyday use." This, too, works to make the conceit more affecting and frightening. If the film involved a big to-do about how newfangled this was, and how some thought it sacrilegious, and others wonderfully futuristic—well, it would be a very different film.

22   Dargis, Manohla. "The Latest in Elective Surgery Will Relieve You of That Nagging Soul," in *The New York Times*, Aug. 7, 2009, p. C8.
23   Lane, Anthony. "The Current Cinema: Lightened Loads," in *The New Yorker* (Aug. 10, 2009), accessed November 1, 2012.

So, here we have one idea about fantasy: Change only one thing, and treat it as no big deal—an absurd premise with a straight face. If you don't want to create a world that's new in every imaginable way, think about changing only one thing. In my case, that would mean that even though this incredible futuristic capacity exists—by pressing a button and a country code, my mind could go off to Argentina, *and it would feel like I was really there*—everything else is as ordinary as ever: I still have to haul luggage, I still don't speak the language, I still get mugged on the street because I'm wandering around like a lost tourist.

To me, it's actually more challenging to invent a world like this, with only one fantastical element, than a world where you can bend reality at will. This, for me, is a kind of metaphor for writing fiction itself: People sometimes say, "Oh, it must be nice to be able to invent everything," but in fact, even though fiction involves making stuff up, as you know by this point, it's full of rules and guidelines, the violation of which will result in bad, uninteresting writing. Fiction is highly restricted rather than a free-for-all. Forcing yourself to imagine a universe where one key thing is different is a version of the same.

CHALLENGE EXERCISE:

Write the story in full.

CRIME OR HORROR?

Purpose: To expand our familiarity with different literary genres.

This week, we'll experiment with other literary genres, specifically crime and horror stories.

Before we get to your assignment, we'll spend some time thinking about the conventions of each. Settle in; it's going to be a while before we get to the actual writing.

If you like to read crime stories and/or horror stories, you might already have some sense of what those conventions are. Are you a fan? Take a crack at listing them yourself. That is, try to come up with three things to say about crime stories and horror stories each. Use the following questions as prompts:

1. How is a crime/horror story different from a "regular" story?

2. What typically happens in a crime/horror story?

3. Are there any differences in writing style, or voice, between crime/horror stories and "regular" stories?

4. What kind of characters tend to appear in crime/horror stories?

5. In what kind of settings do crime/horror stories tend to take place?

Your turn. (And if you've *never* read crime or horror fiction, skip this part and go on to my explanation below.)

Crime:

1. _____

2. _____

3. _____

Horror:

1. _____

2. _____

3. _____

Now for my take:

Crime. Crime stories have lots of sub-genres: The whodunit, the detective story, the thriller, the mystery. (Some of these overlap, of course.) Often, they feature an investigator or private eye—the crime-solver Sherlock Holmes, created by Arthur Conan Doyle (you may know him better from the recent films, starring Robert Downey, Jr. and Jude Law), for instance—engaged in the solution of a crime, or an unraveling of some kind of secret. It's no accident crime stories tend to be bestsellers at the bookstore: Suspense is the name of the game. Who killed old Mrs. Landry? Or: Will Chief Everhart catch the man (or woman!) who killed Mrs. Landry? We might not even get to know or care about Mrs. Landry—just give us a killer and a pursuer, or a mystery about whodunnit, and we're hooked.

Of course, some crime authors go further and make us care about Mrs. Landry, too. This deepens our experience of the story. Crime stories that take care to develop three-dimensional characters with aspirations, flaws, and qualities that make you cringe or root for them, are considered *literary* crime stories, because they borrow from the conventions of literary drama. Because many crime authors *don't* develop their characters a great deal—they might be pure good, or pure evil, not very nuanced—crime tends to be regarded as a less literary genre than drama. But it doesn't have to be. Works by literary crime authors such as James Ellroy and Elmore Leonard are every bit as compelling as (sometimes much more so than) regular old drama. For a comparison between "literary" crime stories and ordinary ones, compare stories by Elmore Leonard and, say, Tom Clancy. It isn't only the characters who are more complex and lifelike in a literary crime story. The language is richer, more surprising, more original too.

At the end of the day, however, literary crime stories and ordinary crime stories share a lot, too. They share the essential characteristic that makes crime stories crime stories: **There's some kind of mystery, or crime, at the heart of the plot.** There's a lot of detail lavished on the setting of the mystery/crime—a shadowy underworld; the mob; CIA operatives in a foreign land—but not so much on the ordinary world around it. (This creates the sensation of existing in an alternate universe.) Everyday people and pursuits tend not to figure as more than wallpaper, in other words invisible surroundings. This is the opposite of Sophie Barthes' approach described in last week's exercise. She takes care to describe the "ordinary" world in as much detail as the genre one.

Some crime authors are challenging this tradition, however; for instance, in 2007 Michael Chabon published *The Yiddish Policemen's Union*, a book that actually combines fantasy with crime. It re-imagines recent international history: Instead of settling in Israel, Jewish émigrés from Europe settle in Alaska, where the U.S. government has granted them a homeland. (That's the fantasy element.) The story revolves around the detective Meyer Landsman, who has to solve a murder. The action takes place in low-lit, seedy cafeterias and basements in what feels like the constant dark. (That's the crime element.) The writing in the book is gorgeous. (That makes it literary.) And the characters are developed far beyond their professional duties. Meyer, for instance, has a complicated relationship with his ex-wife Bina (who also happens to be his boss).

Horror. What makes a horror story a horror story? Well, it's probably scary—for characters and readers both. The atmosphere and setting are spooky—a haunted house, an abandoned motel, a lake in the dark—and features the kind of suspense that drives you to the edge of your seat. (Will the main character survive?) Character-wise, horror stories usually feature some kind of aggressor—sometimes human, sometimes not—and some kind of potential victim, which may be an individual or the entire human race. Or not: They might feature, instead, some kind of dreadful secret the solution of which brings the **protagonist** (the main character of the story) deeper and deeper into some kind of frightening situation.

Instead of generalizing further, let's actually look closely together at a classic horror short story, Edgar Allan Poe's "The Cask of Amontillado." I reproduce it for you below. Please read it, and then we'll discuss. The story, first published in 1846, features some unfamiliar words; first, read through this handy glossary.

- **Amontillado:** a dry sherry

- **Catacombs:** an underground series of tunnels where dead bodies are laid out in recesses

- **Cavern:** underground chamber

- **Conical Cap and Bells:** refers to a jester's outfit

- **Connoisseurship:** expertise

- **Flacon:** a small, decorative bottle

- **Flambeaux:** a lit torch

- **Immolation:** destruction

- **Impunity:** freedom from harm

- **In pace requiescat:** rest in peace

- **Mason:** one who works with stone or brick; also, a member of a secret brotherhood called the Freemasons. (Poe uses this double meaning in the story.)

- **Medoc:** a red wine

- **Nemo me impune lacessit:** no one attacks me with impunity

- **Nitre:** potassium nitrate; a mineral used in the production of explosives

- **Palazzo:** palace

- **Pipe:** a cask of wine, or a container used to hold liquid

- **Roquelaire:** a knee-length cloak

- **Unredressed:** not corrected

- **Virtuoso:** one who is highly skilled[24]

---

24 Glossary courtesy of the site http://nikolledoolin.com/alo/?p=422.

The Cask of Amontillado

by Edgar Allan Poe[25]

The thousand injuries of Fortunato I had borne as I best could; but when he ventured upon insult, I vowed revenge. You, who so well know the nature of my soul, will not suppose, however, that I gave utterance to a threat. *At length* I would be avenged; this was a point definitively settled—but the very definitiveness with which it was resolved, precluded the idea of risk. I must not only punish, but punish with impunity. A wrong is unredressed when retribution overtakes its redresser. It is equally unredressed when the avenger fails to make himself felt as such to him who has done the wrong.

It must be understood, that neither by word nor deed had I given Fortunato cause to doubt my good will. I continued, as was my wont, to smile in his face, and he did not perceive that my smile *now* was at the thought of his immolation.

He had a weak point—this Fortunato—although in other regards he was a man to be respected and even feared. He prided himself on his connoisseurship in wine. Few Italians have the true virtuoso spirit. For the most part their enthusiasm is adopted to suit the time and opportunity—to practise imposture upon the British and Austrian *millionaires*. In painting and gemmary Fortunato, like his countrymen, was a quack—but in the matter of old wines he was sincere. In this respect I did not differ from him materially: I was skilful in the Italian vintages myself, and bought largely whenever I could.

It was about dusk, one evening during the supreme madness of the carnival season, that I encountered my friend. He accosted me with excessive warmth, for he had been drinking much. The man wore motley. He had on a tight-fitting parti-striped dress, and his head was surmounted by the conical cap and bells. I was so pleased to see him, that I thought I should never have done wringing his hand.

I said to him—"My dear Fortunato, you are luckily met. How remarkably well you are looking to-day! But I have received a pipe of what passes for Amontillado, and I have my doubts."

---

25 From *Godey's Lady's Book* (vol. XXXIII, no. 5), November 1846, 33:216-218. If you need some assistance as you read, you may want to read the story on the site http://www2.ivcc.edu/rambo/poe1.htm which provides clarifying comments as you go.

"How?" said he. "Amontillado? A pipe? Impossible! And in the middle of the carnival!"

"I have my doubts," I replied; "and I was silly enough to pay the full Amontillado price without consulting you in the matter. You were not to be found, and I was fearful of losing a bargain."

"Amontillado!"

"I have my doubts."

"Amontillado!"

"And I must satisfy them."

"Amontillado!"

"As you are engaged, I am on my way to Luchesi. If anyone has a critical turn, it is he. He will tell me—"

"Luchesi cannot tell Amontillado from Sherry."

"And yet some fools will have it that his taste is a match for your own."

"Come, let us go."

"Whither?"

"To your vaults."

"My friend, no; I will not impose upon your good nature. I perceive you have an engagement. Luchesi—"

"I have no engagement; —come."

"My friend, no. It is not the engagement, but the severe cold with which I perceive you are afflicted. The vaults are insufferably damp. They are encrusted with nitre."

"Let us go, nevertheless. The cold is merely nothing. Amontillado! You have been imposed upon. And as for Luchesi, he cannot distinguish Sherry from Amontillado."

Thus speaking, Fortunato possessed himself of my arm. Putting on a mask of black silk, and drawing a *roquelaire* closely about my person, I suffered him to hurry me to my palazzo.

There were no attendants at home; they had absconded to make merry in honor of the time. I had told them that I should not return until the morning, and had given them explicit orders not to stir from the house. These orders were sufficient, I well knew, to insure their immediate disappearance, one and all, as soon as my back was turned.

I took from their sconces two flambeaux, and giving one to Fortunato, bowed him through several suites of rooms to the archway that led into the vaults. I passed down a long and winding staircase, requesting him to be cautious as he followed. We came at length to the foot of the descent, and stood together on the damp ground of the catacombs of the Montresors.

The gait of my friend was unsteady, and the bells upon his cap jingled as he strode.

"The pipe," he said.

"It is farther on," said I; "but observe the white web-work which gleams from these cavern walls."

He turned towards me, and looked into my eyes with two filmy orbs that distilled the rheum of intoxication.

"Nitre?" he asked, at length.

"Nitre," I replied. "How long have you had that cough?"

"Ugh! ugh! ugh! —ugh! Ugh! ugh! —ugh! ugh! ugh! —ugh! ugh! ugh! —ugh! ugh! ugh!"

My poor friend found it impossible to reply for many minutes.

"It is nothing," he said, at last.

"Come," I said, with decision, "we will go back; your health is precious. You are rich, respected, admired, beloved; you are happy, as once I was. You are a man to be missed. For me it is no matter. We will go back; you will be ill, and I cannot be responsible. Besides, there is Luchesi—"

"Enough," he said; "the cough is a mere nothing; it will not kill me. I shall not die of a cough."

"True—true," I replied; "and, indeed, I had no intention of alarming you unnecessarily— but you should use all proper caution. A draught of this Medoc will defend us from the damps."

Here I knocked off the neck of a bottle which I drew from a long row of its fellows that lay upon the mould.

"Drink," I said, presenting him the wine.

He raised it to his lips with a leer. He paused and nodded to me familiarly, while his bells jingled.

"I drink," he said, "to the buried that repose around us."

"And I to your long life."

He again took my arm, and we proceeded.

"These vaults," he said, "are extensive."

"The Montresors," I replied, "were a great and numerous family."

"I forget your arms."

"A huge human foot d'or, in a field azure; the foot crushes a serpent rampant whose fangs are imbedded in the heel."

"And the motto?"

"*Nemo me impune lacessit.*"

"Good!" he said.

The wine sparkled in his eyes and the bells jingled. My own fancy grew warm with the Medoc. We had passed through walls of piled bones, with casks and puncheons intermingling, into the inmost recesses of the catacombs. I paused again, and this time I made bold to seize Fortunato by an arm above the elbow.

"The nitre!" I said; "see, it increases. It hangs like moss upon the vaults. We are below the river's bed. The drops of moisture trickle among the bones. Come, we will go back ere it is too late. Your cough—"

"It is nothing," he said; "let us go on. But first, another draught of the Medoc."

I broke and reached him a flacon of De Grâve. He emptied it at a breath. His eyes flashed with a fierce light. He laughed and threw the bottle upwards with a gesticulation

I did not understand.

I looked at him in surprise. He repeated the movement—a grotesque one.

"You do not comprehend?" he said.

"Not I," I replied.

"Then you are not of the brotherhood."

"How?"

"You are not of the masons."

"Yes, yes," I said, "yes, yes."

"You? Impossible! A mason?"

"A mason," I replied.

"A sign," he said.

"It is this," I answered, producing a trowel from beneath the folds of my *roquelaire*.

"You jest," he exclaimed, recoiling a few paces. "But let us proceed to the Amontillado."

"Be it so," I said, replacing the tool beneath the cloak, and again offering him my arm. He leaned upon it heavily. We continued our route in search of the Amontillado. We passed through a range of low arches, descended, passed on, and descending again, arrived at a deep crypt, in which the foulness of the air caused our flambeaux rather to glow than flame.

At the most remote end of the crypt there appeared another less spacious. Its walls had been lined with human remains, piled to the vault overhead, in the fashion of the great catacombs of Paris. Three sides of this interior crypt were still ornamented in this manner. From the fourth the bones had been thrown down, and lay promiscuously upon the earth, forming at one point a mound of some size. Within the wall thus exposed by the displacing of the bones, we perceived a still interior recess, in depth about four feet, in width three, in height six or seven. It seemed to have been constructed for no especial use within itself, but formed merely the interval between two of the colossal supports of the roof of the catacombs, and was backed by one of their circumscribing walls of solid granite.

It was in vain that Fortunato, uplifting his dull torch, endeavored to pry into the depth of the recess. Its termination the feeble light did not enable us to see.

"Proceed," I said; "herein is the Amontillado. As for Luchesi—"

"He is an ignoramus," interrupted my friend, as he stepped unsteadily forward, while I followed immediately at his heels. In an instant he had reached the extremity of the niche, and finding his progress arrested by the rock, stood stupidly bewildered. A moment more and I had fettered him to the granite. In its surface were two iron staples, distant from each other about two feet, horizontally. From one of these depended a short chain, from the other a padlock. Throwing the links about his waist, it was but the work of a few seconds to secure it. He was too much astounded to resist. Withdrawing the key I stepped back from the recess.

"Pass your hand," I said, "over the wall; you cannot help feeling the nitre. Indeed, it is *very* damp. Once more let me *implore* you to return. No? Then I must positively leave you. But I must first render you all the little attentions in my power."

"The Amontillado!" ejaculated my friend, not yet recovered from his astonishment.

"True," I replied; "the Amontillado."

As I said these words I busied myself among the pile of bones of which I have before spoken. Throwing them aside, I soon uncovered a quantity of building stone and mortar. With these materials and with the aid of my trowel, I began vigorously to wall up the entrance of the niche.

I had scarcely laid the first tier of the masonry when I discovered that the intoxication of Fortunato had in a great measure worn off. The earliest indication I had of this was a low moaning cry from the depth of the recess. It was *not* the cry of a drunken man. There was then a long and obstinate silence. I laid the second tier, and the third, and the fourth; and then I heard the furious vibrations of the chain. The noise lasted for several minutes, during which, that I might hearken to it with the more satisfaction, I ceased my labors and sat down upon the bones. When at last the clanking subsided, I resumed the trowel, and finished without interruption the fifth, the sixth, and the seventh tier. The wall was now nearly upon a level with my breast. I again paused, and holding the flambeaux over the mason-work, threw a few feeble rays upon the figure within.

A succession of loud and shrill screams, bursting suddenly from the throat of the chained form, seemed to thrust me violently back. For a brief moment I hesitated—I trembled. Unsheathing my rapier, I began to grope with it about the recess: but the thought of an instant reassured me. I placed my hand upon the solid fabric of the catacombs, and felt satisfied. I reapproached the wall. I replied to the yells of him who clamored. I re-echoed—I aided—I surpassed them in volume and in strength. I did this, and the clamorer grew still.

It was now midnight, and my task was drawing to a close. I had completed the eighth, the ninth, and the tenth tier. I had finished a portion of the last and the eleventh; there remained but a single stone to be fitted and plastered in. I struggled with its weight; I placed it partially in its destined position. But now there came from out the niche a low laugh that erected the hairs upon my head. It was succeeded by a sad voice, which I had difficulty in recognising as that of the noble Fortunato. The voice said—

"Ha! ha! ha! —he! he! —a very good joke indeed—an excellent jest. We will have many a rich laugh about it at the palazzo—he! he! He! —over our wine—he! he! he!"

"The Amontillado!" I said.

"He! he! he! —he! he! he! —yes, the Amontillado. But is it not getting late? Will not they be awaiting us at the palazzo, the Lady Fortunato and the rest? Let us be gone."

"Yes," I said, "let us be gone."

"For the love of God, Montresor!"

"Yes," I said, "for the love of God!"

But to these words I hearkened in vain for a reply. I grew impatient. I called aloud—

"Fortunato!"

No answer. I called again—

"Fortunato!"

No answer still. I thrust a torch through the remaining aperture and let it fall within. There came forth in return only a jingling of the bells. My heart grew sick—on account of the dampness of the catacombs. I hastened to make an end of my labor. I forced the last stone into its position; I plastered it up. Against the new masonry I re-erected the old rampart of bones. For the half of a century no mortal has disturbed them.

In pace requiescat!

*

So, where does the horror come from in this story? Not from an attack by an assailant, or from suspense about whether the protagonist will survive. But suspense there is plenty. The story opens with—think back to our discussions of structure—some backstory (the first three paragraphs). The narrator, Montresor, has endured an unnamed insult from the aggressor Fortunato, and is bent on exacting his revenge. We, in turn, become bent on finding out: What will it be?

As Montresor leads Fortunato into his wine vault—ostensibly to have him certify a cask of wine as the real deal rather than a fake, taking care to flatter him all the way, as well as regularly insist they turn back on account of Fortunato's cold and the vault's dampness—our dread deepens. What will he do to Fortunato? The setting helps: A crypt with bones and remains.

Before our worst suspicions are confirmed—Montresor walls up Fortunato alive—we might think about something I discussed in the last volume of *The Creative Writer* series: The **anti-hero** protagonist. Our natural tendency, as readers, is to ally ourselves with the person telling the story—he or she is our guide. Plus, Montresor has endured some kind of insult from Fortunato, so that only endears us to him more. But

Montresor ends up committing a heinous act, complicating our feelings about him, to say the least. Meanwhile, Fortunato is apparently someone who thinks nothing of insulting Montresor over and over, and is vain, to boot—he enjoys having his wine skills flattered, and in fact, it's the challenge of determining the authenticity of the cask of Amontillado that causes him to suspend judgment and blunder along with a man who isn't too fond of him. You could say his vanity blinds his wits. All the same, does he deserve the fate he receives? We leave the story with a great deal of ambivalence about both men, and perhaps a bit of chill borrowed from those nitre-encrusted walls.

By the way, "The Cask of Amontillado" may be based on historical fact. When Poe was in the army, he was stationed in a fort in Boston Harbor where he learned a terrible story: Ten years before, a beloved young officer was killed by an older one in a sword duel because they had had a disagreement over cards. To avenge the murder, the younger officer's friends captured the older man and walled him up alive in a crypt. To me, this story is even more terrifying than what Poe did with it—moving the action to Italy, with wine aficionados—because violence by a group is often more scary than by a single individual.

Your assignment: Now that you've looked at the principles of crime and horror, do for either a crime or horror story what you did last week for a fantasy story: Story idea, rough plot, characters, 500-word scene.[26]

CHALLENGE EXERCISES:

1. If you worked on a crime story, work on a horror story, and vice versa.

2. Continue your study of literary genre. Wikipedia provides a handy introduction to some of the main ones—just type "literary genre" into the search engine. Which ones are the most interesting to you?

3. Continue your study of horror, crime, and fantasy stories.

---

26   If you're going to work on a crime story, you may find of interest an entry titled "Twenty rules for writing detective stories," written by the early-20th-century crime author Willard Huntington Wright in 1928 and available at http://gaslight.mtroyal.ca/vandine.htm.

The list of horror masters is long: Edgar Allan Poe, Stephen King, Bram Stoker (*Dracula*), Robert Louis Stevenson (*The Strange Case of Dr. Jekyll and Mr. Hyde*), Mary Shelley (*Frankenstein*), H. P. Lovecraft. As you read, think about what conventions these authors share; which they don't; and, most importantly, how they tinker with the conventions of horror storytelling. To answer these questions, think about the 5 Essentials and the prompt questions that appear in the last two lessons.

For crime, you have just as many options. One starting place might be the anthology *Classic Crime Short Stories*, widely available as an audiobook. Here you'll get a sampling of crime writing by authors who also happen to be literary greats, such as Graham Greene. If you're looking for longer-length work, you can hardly do better than Dashiell Hammett, who took crime and mystery writing in this country to a new level in the 1920s. His successor Raymond Chandler is also renowned. Agatha Christie (*And Then there Were None*, one of the best-selling books of all time, with 100 million copies sold) and Edgar Allan Poe ("Murders in the Rue Morgue," by some accounts the first detective story ever written) are other examples.

Fantasy seems all the rage right now in the literary world, so you'll have no trouble finding examples of it, from the *Twilight* series to *Harry Potter* to *The Lord of the Rings* trilogy, and so on. Sometimes, the classics do just as well if not better: As mentioned above, these include *The Chronicles of Narnia* by C. S. Lewis, *The Wizard of Oz* by L. Frank Baum, and so on. Keep your notion of fantasy broad—the *Terminator* movies are fantasy; so is another famous Arnold Schwarzenegger project: *Total Recall*. And all this is without touching on a huge sub-genre of fantasy, namely science fiction: Isaac Asimov (*Foundation* series), Orson Scott Card (*Ender's Game*), H. G. Wells (*The Time Machine*).

FICTION • SECTION 7

FORMAT

NON-LINEAR DIALOGUE

Purpose: To refine our dialogue skills as we prepare to try our hand at plays and screenplays.

In the weeks that follow, you will try your hand at other writing formats—or genres, if you will—specifically a play. If you've noticed, we've been talking about movies as often as prose. Part of the reason for that is my interest in cinema, but part of it has to do with the overlap between fiction and both plays and films, especially when it comes to dialogue.

In our lessons together, you may have picked up on another reason: The value of experimenting with other voices, perspectives, genres, and formats goes beyond learning something new. You learn something old as well—by which I mean that working with a new format often teaches you just as much about the voice/perspective/genre/format you were working in previously.

For instance, plays make far less use of shifting settings than fiction, because they are meant to be performed live, and there are only so many times stagehands can change the scenery. By downplaying setting, plays can help you realize, in contrast, just how much meaning settings have in typical fiction.

Both plays and screenplays make use of far more dialogue than fiction does. Have you ever seen the text of a play or screenplay in print? It's 90% dialogue, with some **stage directions**—clarifying instructions about the setting, the mood, the action—thrown in. So, experimenting with these formats over the next several weeks will force us to study dialogue more deeply.

We'll start out this week with a preparatory lesson on dialogue alone. Next week, we'll dive into plays.

Our first assignment: **Non-linear dialogue**. That's my way of referring to the way people speak *past* each other. To see what I mean, read the following (invented) dialogue between two characters:

Character One: What did you do yesterday?

Character Two: I am so tired. I could fall asleep standing up. I heard elephants do that.

One: But then you'd be really fat.

Two: I could scoop things up with my nose.

One: They'd sell your tusks on the black market.

Two: When they had the tornado in Missouri, they brought in an elephant to dig through the wreckage.

One: Are you going to finish that toast?

Two: That elephant looked so sad digging through people's couches. Maybe he found some change.

One: It's so warm outside!

Two: Yeah, you can have the toast. I'm too tired to eat.

What did you notice about this dialogue? Note how in the first pair of lines, Character Two responds to the question of what she did yesterday, but not literally—"Yesterday, I did x, y, and z." Whatever she did yesterday made her very tired, so she says *that*. Or maybe she's not thinking about yesterday at all, even though Character One is asking about it. Whatever her friend wants to talk about, Two's mind is occupied by the fact that she's tired.

That, in turn, makes her exaggerate by saying that she could fall asleep standing up, which reminds her of having heard that elephants do that. All of a sudden, a conversation about Two's activities yesterday shifts to elephants.

Again, Two doesn't respond to One directly. One says, "You'd be really fat." Instead of saying "yes" or "no" or saying something about weight, Two mentions something else she could do as an elephant. One responds fairly directly, continuing to talk about tusks, but again, Two is off on her own tangent about an elephant helping the clean-up after a tornado in Missouri. That is, the same thread—elephants—runs through most of this dialogue, but the two speakers are more or less having their own conversations, though with each other.

Then One steers the conversation away from elephants by asking about the toast. Two is still on that scene in Missouri. Even though she hasn't gotten an answer, One moves away from her own conversation (about toast) to remark on the weather. Belatedly, Two responds about the toast. (Haven't you had that happen, when something someone said lingers in your mind until you finally respond to it a minute later?)

My aim in this dialogue was to point out how indirectly we communicate with each other. Often, we think about our own problems, having conversations with ourselves while conversing with someone else, steering the conversation to what we *really* want to talk about.

We do this for many reasons. Maybe we have a crush on the other person and are trying not to let on. Or we may feel guilty for being angry at the person we're speaking to. In both cases, our feelings probably come out in our tone, anyway. (Often, the other person will be responding to the tone, rather than our words.) Or perhaps we have an actual secret we're keeping from the other person. Or simply, we're not that interested in what the other person is saying, but feel obligated to keep up the conversation—because it's Grandma, or an elder, or a person in authority.

A conversation is a dance between what's really on our mind, how nice or acceptable or relevant to the conversation that is, and what we actually say. Dialogue has to reflect that. By contrast, a conversation like this sounds stilted and unreal, doesn't it?

One: What did you do yesterday?

Two: Yesterday, I woke up at seven, cleaned my room, did my homework, watered the flowers, and ran the dog.

One: Not a bad day's work.

Two: No, it wasn't a bad day's work.

One: You must feel pretty good about yourself.

Two: I feel pretty good about myself.

Doesn't it sound like Two is a robot? Well, she's responding literally to what is being said to her. People don't tend to do that.

How did I come up with the non-linear dialogue higher up? I didn't plan it out in advance. I came up with a first sentence and decided to see what clues it could give me. So, the first line has One asking how yesterday went for Two. I knew that Two wouldn't respond directly. But in what way would she respond indirectly? I decided she would say something about what yesterday was *like* for her, as opposed to saying what exactly she did yesterday. What was it like? I wondered. Let's say she's tired. That made me think of something I had heard about elephants—that they sleep standing up. And then Two's mention of elephants gave me an idea what One could say in the next line.

If you were to categorize the kinds of responses that appear throughout the exchange, you might count at least three:

1. **Belated response:** "Yeah, you can have the toast" is responding to something that was said several comments before.

2. **Non-response:** "That elephant looked so sad…" is responding to something Two herself said earlier rather than what One has just asked.

3. **Tangential response:** "I could scoop things up with my nose" keeps on the general subject of elephants but doesn't respond directly to the remark "Then you'd be really fat."

Today, you'll write 500 words of your own non-linear dialogue.

Here's a useful preliminary exercise, a reworking of an exercise that appeared in the second volume of *The Creative Writer* series. Record, and then transcribe, an ordinary dialogue between family members. (If you have an audio recorder, just bring it down to dinner and turn it on before the meal and off after. It's your call whether to alert your family members that you're recording them. When they don't know they're being recorded, people tend to speak more casually.) After you've transcribed a brief chunk of the recorded dialogue, pay attention to the way both of the people in the conversation probably are not answering each other in the stilted, literal way presented above in the lesson. What you might start to realize is that it's actually the norm to speak slightly "past" each other in this way all the time.

If that's the case, you might ask, why practice it? Because the way we speak and the way we *write* speech are very different. When beginning writers start writing dialogue, its worst sin is usually that it's very stilted. It's as if some kind of "formal" switch turns on and our characters start speaking in complete sentences, with perfect grammar, and in direct response to what was said to them—definitely NOT the way people speak in real life. So an author, as strange as it sounds, has to re-create the awkwardness and indirectness with which people speak to each other.

It takes some time and practice to develop a feel for this, so don't be frustrated if you struggle with it in this lesson. Your assignment is to cook up something that's supposed to sound as if it wasn't cooked up at all—that's hard. But here are some pointers:

- Imagine yourself not as the author of the scene or the story but as one of the characters. Imagine someone—a parent, a sibling, or a friend—asking you "What did you do yesterday?" It's okay if your instinct is to start answering by answering directly—say, "I went to the Laundromat with my mom." But chances are the Laundromat is going to make you think of something that took place there, or something that jumped into your mind while you were waiting for the laundry to finish, and so the next thing you say is likely to be less direct.

- Latch on to a specific word in the first character's statement and run with that instead. For instance, in response to "What did you do yesterday," the second character might say: "Yesterday, today, tomorrow, it's all the same. I haven't been out of bed in days. This flu is going to be the end of me."

- Another idea: If the first character has asked a question, the second character can ignore it, or respond without answering it. Person 1: "What did you do yesterday?" Person 2: "It's so hot today I want to climb in a freezer."

- Keep in mind that the dialogue shouldn't go out of its way to be non-linear. That would become silly, trying too hard in the opposite direction. People do respond to each other, as you saw in the dialogue example that started the lesson, just not in all cases directly and immediately.

- Lean on your mentor for help through role-playing. Ask the mentor to give you a line, or give him or her one. When it's your turn to respond, say something non-linear. Non-linear response actually isn't easy to highlight when you're trying consciously; observing others in dialogue tends to be much more effective.

- An advance peek at one of your challenge exercises: Pick up a favorite short story and make a list of the ways in which the dialogue is non-linear (belated, non-response, tangential, etc.) That can serve as a model for your own dialogue, the goal being to have an equal number of examples of each of the three types. Then, once you have your first line of dialogue, you might say to yourself: What would be a tangential response here? Or a non-response? (In order for the response to be belated, it couldn't appear in the second line.) Then you might ask yourself: Why is it a tangential/non-response? That is, what is this character actually thinking about? The answer to that question might provide a bit more material for you to work with as you make your way through the dialogue, a background narrative to supply some of the non-direct comments. It becomes easier the further you get.

Your assignment: Pick two characters and write 500 words of non-linear dialogue between them. Do as many of the preliminary steps above as necessary.

CHALLENGE EXERCISES:

1. Take dialogue you've written previously and re-write it to be more non-linear.

2. Re-read a favorite short story, paying close attention to the way in which the speakers do and don't respond to each other directly. You can try to classify non-linear responses as one of the three types mentioned above: Belated response, non-response, tangential response.

3. Spend the week of this exercise listening to this aspect of dialogue in particular as you listen to the way people speak. You'll be amazed by the ways we all speak past each other most of the time.

LET'S WRITE A PLAY, PART I

Purpose: To familiarize ourselves with some of the conventions of playwriting.

This two-week section will have you practice dialogue in a whole new way—through the reading of a play, and the writing of a scene in one of your own.

How does storytelling in a play differ from a short story? Some of the answers are obvious. In a short story, the narrator can provide some backstory to help the reader make sense of what's going on. Just look at the opening three paragraphs of "The Cask of Amontillado" in Week 13. If you've ever seen a play, you'll have noticed that there isn't a mechanism to supply the audience with this kind of backstory—it's just not one of the conventions. And so the dialogue between the characters has to, little by little, make clear to the audience what exactly is going on. (*The Creative Writer, Level Two* features a lesson called "Dialogue as Plot.")

As you'll notice in the play we read together this week, a lot of information about what's going on comes from **stage directions**. These are the directions given to the actors, the set designers, and the costume designers by the playwright.

As mentioned last week, plays make use of changing settings far less than fiction or films—there are only so many times stage hands can swap out the background, and only so many sets a play's producers are willing to finance. But that's not to say that setting plays less of a role—in fact, quite possibly more, because it doesn't change for long stretches of the performance.

That said, setting in theatres is rarely as elaborate as in fiction or films. Very often, the stage direction won't go beyond something like "a small room in a beat-up hotel." How a set designer chooses to bring that to life has many possibilities, but chances are you'll see a ratty bed, a dusty floor, and a window framed by a peeling pane—in other words, a suggestion toward a setting rather than much of a setting. In a play even more than in a short story, the focus is on the characters and what they have to say to each other.

What else do plays feature? Costumes, lighting, and sound. Of course, the clothing worn by the characters in a short story is significant, too, but because plays are meant to be performed live, the costumes take on even greater importance. More or less the same thing can be said about sound. Lighting is one element entirely unshared by short stories, because lighting is limited to live performance.

Another difference is that plays don't deal with point of view in the same way that short stories do. Usually, there isn't a narrator telling the story—the story just unfolds in front of you, the only narrator-like hints coming from the stage directions.

But one thing that plays absolutely do share with short stories is their emphasis on plot. "Drama is like a boxing match," in the words of playwright Lavonne Mueller.[27] "Drama is the art of the showdown," says theater director Louis Catron.[28] In other words, just as an author has to interest readers in turning the page, a playwright has to interest readers in staying in the seat. He or she does so in the same way a fiction author does: Getting the viewer to care about the situation the characters find themselves in, and wondering how they'll come out of it. As Mueller says, "In the musical *A Chorus Line*, the plot/dramatic question is simply: Who will get chosen for the chorus line?"[29] Of course, viewers won't stay in their seats if they don't care about the characters, if the writing is plain, and if the work suffers from the other pitfalls that threaten a story or a play. But posing this kind of suspense is a good start.

This week, we'll start by having a look at the basics of a published play, "The Long Christmas Dinner" by Thornton Wilder; your first assignment is to find it in the local

27   Mueller, Lavonne. "The S-N-A-P-P-E-R Test for Playwrights," in *The Writer's Handbook*, ed. Sylvia K. Burack, The Writer, Inc., 1987, p. 412.
28   Catron, Louis E. "Guidelines for the Beginning Playwright," in *The Writer's Handbook*, ed. Sylvia K. Burack, The Writer, Inc., 1987, p. 433.
29   Mueller, p. 413.

library. I recommend you read this one-act play twice—once simply to understand what happens and the second time to appreciate its nuances more closely. While short, the play is rich and tricky—90 years pass in 27 pages, with several generations of the Bayard family passing across the stage. (You may wish to draw a family tree, along with notes on what happens to each character, to make things easier.) Because so much happens, dialogue and stage direction has to do that much more in making clear to the reader what's going on. That's part of the reason I wanted to use this play. I used *The Long Christmas Dinner and Other Plays in One Act*, in an Avon/Bard Books edition from 1980, but it can be found in other collections as well.

Your assignment: Below is a series of questions. Answer them yourself before looking at my answers. And don't just "answer" them in your head. Either tell the answers to your mentor, or jot down a few sentences for each.

If you're completely baffled by a question or two, go ahead and look at my answer--but then be sure to find more examples of what I describe, since I only provide one or two per question.

1. **What is the play about, at its most basic?**

2. **Who are the main characters? What happens to each, and when?**

3. **Name some time markers in the play.**

4. **Let's discuss the stage directions. What do they tell us?**

5. **What costumes/props are used to indicate the passage of time/progress in plot?**

6. **How do we learn backstory, and what is it?**

7. **What are some of the most notable things about the dialogue?**

8. **How do we learn about the setting?**

Now for my answers:

1. What is the play about, at its most basic?

A: The play tells the story of the Bayard family over the course of nearly a century through its Christmas dinners.

2. Who are the main characters? What happens to each, and when?

A: The play opens with the matriarch, Mother Bayard, and her children Roderick and Lucia. Roderick and Lucia have a son named Charles and a daughter named Genevieve. Genevieve remains unmarried. Charles marries Leonora, with whom he has three children: Roderick, Lucia, and Sam. Sam dies in the war, leaving Roderick and Lucia—namesakes of the two characters who started the play. Other characters include Cousin Brandon, Cousin Ermengarde, and a constantly changing cast of servants.

3. Name some time markers in the play.

A: We get the very first one on page 2: "Our first Christmas dinner in the new house." This is an example, as well, of **dialogue as plot**: Ostensibly, Roderick is expressing excitement about being in a new home. But he's simultaneously tipping off readers about where and when the play is taking place. You might remember this as "**omeletting**" —the author "folds" into the exclamation the news that we're in a new home on Christmas.

Two pages later, Mother Bayard says: "Five years… This is your sixth Christmas dinner."

And just another page later, without the audience having ever been told that Mother Bayard has died, Lucia makes it clear by omeletting: "I can't forget her sitting in her wheelchair right beside us, only a year ago." Thus, we know she's dead, and this must be the seventh Christmas dinner in the house.

By page 8, Roderick and Lucia have had a son, Charles, already "twelve" (again, revealed indirectly). And so on.

4. Let's discuss the stage directions. What do they tell us?

A: A page-plus of stage directions opens the play and tells us a bit about what we need to know: where we are, what the play will show us, what the actors need to keep in mind as they perform, and how the props are to be used.

5. What costumes/props are used to indicate the passage of time/progress in plot?

A: The most obvious are the wigs and shawls used to signify the characters' advance in age. Of course, the Christmas dinner table itself, with its accoutrements (the serving fork, the wine glasses), are props of their own. In a play more concerned with the general subject of passing time than the particular fates of these particular characters, even the individual characters may be seen as props of a kind—tools used to express the author's ultimate message.

6. How do we learn backstory, and what is it?

A: Our first clue comes on the very first page: "Ninety years are to be traversed in this play…"

7. What are some of the most notable things about the dialogue?

A: As discussed above, despite the detailed stage directions, it's the dialogue that tells the audience the most about the passage of time in the play. (After all, the audience never sees the stage directions.)

Also, the dialogue repeats very often. Over and over, we hear the same phrases ("a little white meat?"; "we need him in our firm"; "every least twig is wrapped around with ice"), the same subjects of discussion (Major Lewis with his ailments, the splendid sermons at the church). While the dialogue works hard to indicate passage of time, it's also monotonous and repetitive—Wilder seems to be making the point that the magic of family isn't in excitement or novelty but stability, tradition, and bonds.

8. How do we learn about the setting?

A: Again, the opening stage directions tell us that we're in "the dining-room of the Bayard home" at a "handsomely spread" Christmas dinner.

Note:
"The Long Christmas Dinner" is a highly **symbolic** play. For instance, the stage portals are meant to symbolize birth and death—to come through the door on stage-left is not to walk into the room (**literalism**) but to be born (**symbolism**). It's not really a realist play—it's not absurd or fantastical, but it's also less about the events described (the

gossip, the family updates, the historical events) than the passage of time symbolized by the unusual conventions of the play (the wigs, the shawls, the stage portals, the rapid passage of time and the rapidly changing cast). Another way to put this would be that the **form** of the play is of more significance than the **content**. (After all, the characters repeat themselves generation in and out.) However, plays hardly have to get into this level of symbolism. Some of the best drama of the 20th century is realist drama—people like you and me, talking in a room.

CHALLENGE EXERCISE:

Learn more about Thornton Wilder, one of America's greatest playwrights in the 20th century. (You can start on Wikipedia.) Read his greatest play, *Our Town*.

WRITING A SCENE FOR A PLAY

Purpose: To continue learning about dialogue in playwriting.

Having picked apart a classic play last week, this week you'll try your hand at a scene for a play of your own. This is primarily a **dialogue** exercise—I want you to practice writing dialogue that gives readers **plot** and **backstory** without sounding contrived. ("Well, Mary, as you know, last year, I was ill…") But you can hardly do this without first answering some of the same questions you would with a short story. I'll prompt you with some below.

1. What's the plot?

2. Who are the characters? How many are there? What do they want?

3. What is the "showdown," or "boxing match," that Lavonne Mueller and Louis Catron ask for? In other words, what's the play's conflict(s)?

4. What will the set look like? Will the setting change during your segment?

5. What will the characters wear?

6. What will they talk about? How will this convey to the audience what the plot is?

7. What will the opening stage directions say? That is, what does the audience need to know about plot, setting, and the characters to be able to make sense of what's going on?

8. Will any particular sounds outside the characters' voices punctuate the action?

9. Are you going to write the opening 500 words of the play, or an excerpt from a later part?

10. If you were a critic writing a review of your own play, what are some of the things you might say (other than that it was spectacular)?

Your assignment: Work on throwing down some ideas in answer to the questions above. When you're finished, write a scene of at least 500 words. Use classic play formatting, which looks like this:

CHARACTER X

This is my first line of dialogue!

 (CHARACTER X does something. This is a stage direction.)

CHARACTER Y

That's fascinating!

 (CHARACTER Y copies CHARACTER X.)

CHARACTER X

I completely agree.

If you want more details on how to properly format a script, there are numerous online sites that can give you more direction, such as: http://www.scriptfrenzy.org/howtoformatastageplay

When you're finished, try reading your scene out loud along with your mentor. How does the dialogue sound to your ear? To your mentor's ear?

Challenge exercises:

1. Re-write your 500 words of play as 500 words in a short story.

2. Can you extend the scene into a complete one-act play? Use "The Long Christmas Dinner" as a guide in terms of story arc, length, pacing, etc.

EXPERIMENTAL FICTION

Purpose: To go beyond plot-driven fiction.

In all four books of this series, I've been encouraging you to think about storytelling as revolving around plot—a character's quest, or some kind of conflict, all in order to entice the reader to wonder what happens next.

But not all stories keep to this notion. Some of the very best stories reject it. I believe it's important to learn the rules before you start breaking them—as the great writing teacher (and novelist) John Gardner said, "No writer should ever have to hesitate for an instant over what the rule to be kept or suspended *is*"[30] —but I think the time has come to talk a little bit about those "rule-breaking" stories.

Some stories and novels "break the rules" more than others. For instance, the South African writer Barry Yourgrau writes what's called **flash fiction**. His stories are very, very short. They're also very unconventional if you're looking for a traditional plot or characters. (His 1987 collection *Wearing Dad's Head* includes stories about a safari in the suburbs and a cow in lingerie.) Same goes for the absurdism of a writer like Daniil Kharms (1905-1942). Here's one of his stories in its entirety:

Falling old ladies
by Daniil Kharms

Because of her excessive curiosity, one old woman tumbled out of her window, fell and shattered to pieces.

---

30 Gardner, p. 17.

Another old woman leaned out to look at the one who'd shattered but, out of excessive curiosity, also tumbled out of her window, fell and shattered to pieces.

Then a third old woman tumbled from her window, and a fourth, and a fifth.
When the sixth old woman tumbled out of her window, I got sick of watching them and walked over to the Maltsev Market where, they said, a blind man had been given a knit shawl.[31]

See what I mean?

Other works look a lot more like conventional stories but in fact don't feature much in the way of a plot. Instead, they center on the experiences of a particular character(s), and the emphasis is less on "what happens next" than on "what kind of a person is this?" Examples include John Kennedy Toole's *A Confederacy of Dunces*, Saul Bellow's *The Adventures of Augie March*, and F. Scott Fitzgerald's *This Side of Paradise*.

31 Kharms, Daniil. "Tumbling Old Women," from *Today I Wrote Nothing: The Selected Writings of Daniil Kharms*, edited and translated by Matvei Yankelevich (New York, NY: The Overlook Press, Peter Mayer Publishers, Inc., 2007), p. 47. Translation copyright 2007 by Matvei Yankelevich.

Still other works devote as much attention to the portrait of a place—setting—as they do to that of character or plot. Willa Cather's *My Ántonia* doesn't have much *plot*, though many things do happen. (Plot refers specifically to the kinds of dramatic twists that make you want to read on.) And the characters left at least this reader somewhat underwhelmed. But Cather's portrait of Nebraska frontier life in the late 19th century is powerful and sharp.

This week, your assignment will be to familiarize yourself with stories and excerpts from works that fall outside the traditional track.

Your assignment: Below, find a handful of candidates. Your job is to choose three and look them up in the library. As you read the works, try to pay special attention to the ways in which the stories ignore the 5 Essentials. For your own development, you may also want to wonder about how that affects your enjoyment of the stories. Do you like them more/less than the more traditional stories I've been having you look at? I don't want you to answer that question right away. Anything strange-seeming is likely to produce a negative reaction, at least initially. Make sure to complete the assignment and let several days go by. Then think about the question again.

Remember to write your thoughts down or tell them to your mentor; don't just formulate them in your head.

Candidates:

1. Barry Yourgrau, "Milk," in *A Man Jumps Out of an Airplane*
2. Jorge Luis Borges, "The Library of Babel," in *Labyrinths*
3. Donald Barthelme, "The School," in *Sixty Stories*
4. Mary Caponegro, "Ill-Timed," in *All Fall Down*
5. Ben Marcus, any of the stories in *The Age of Wire and String*

CHALLENGE EXERCISE:

Try your hand at an experimental work, for instance a short story that, like Daniil Kharms', goes on, in its entirety, for no more than 250 words. In a previous level of this series, I asked the writer to compose a 100-word short story with all the elements of a traditional story: Plot, characters, a story arc, and so forth. Well, this is as an assignment to do the same with none of those restrictions.

You'll find it's not as easy as it sounds. Restrictions—plot, characters, etc.—are useful because they serve as guidelines, helping us populate a frighteningly blank page. You might help yourself by deciding which of the 5 Essentials to dispense with. Perhaps you'd like to spend your 250 words describing the way a glass of juice looks to thirsty eyes after a game of basketball—no plot there, no characters even, just observation. Or maybe you want to experiment by comprising 250 words in which the word "the" never appears. Or a particular letter. (The French novelist George Perec once wrote a whole novel without the letter "e.") Or perhaps you want to write a segment featuring not a fictional character but someone with your name—though it may or may not be you. The options are limitless. If you've ever had a moment this year, or over the past four, where you've wanted to try something but it didn't fit the traditional parameters of the assignment, this is the time to do it. Use the experimental stories you read as a guide to how much you can "fool around."

CONCLUSION

CLOSING SHORT STORY

Purpose: To write a short story that utilizes skills learned in this, and previous, levels, with the aim of submitting it to a literary journal for consideration.

As at the conclusion of every level of *The Creative Writer* series, the semester's final assignment is to compose a story of your own choosing. My hope is that before starting to, you'll review some of the things we've talked about this year—second-person and collective narrators; genres; formats; using action verbs and descriptions instead of adverbs; and so on.

Perhaps you might choose to work on an experimental story longer than last week's 250-word challenge exercise.

Either way, a great way to culminate your work this last year of the series would be to submit your story, after finishing, for consideration by a literary journal. More information about the kinds of publications that publish short stories and poems appears in this volume's appendix. There are also reminders there about the importance of revision, how to put up with rejection (a mainstay of even the best writers' lives), and other aspects of making one's work public.

Or perhaps you don't wish to try to get the story published; that's fine, too. There is no requirement that one write for anyone but oneself, for one's "desk drawer," so to speak. I just thought it might be interesting, after year(s) of composing for oneself and possibly your mentor, to send the story out into the world, to see whether it resonates with others. In either case, there are some words in the appendix about private vs. public writing, and how writing can be of benefit to one's life in either case.

So, you may wish to consult the appendix after finishing the first draft of your story—that is, while it's "cooling" and you need to pass time before revising it with fresh eyes.

POETRY

PREFACE

"A poem is sometimes taught...as if the important thing were to get to the bottom of it, to solve all its mysteries, to analyze everything until all was understood... [But] poetry isn't purely intellectual... With an expository essay, an appropriate first question is, 'Can I understand it?' With a poem (or a story), you ask, 'Is it beautiful? Is it new? Is it moving?'" [32]

In this, the final year of our poetry work together, we'll deepen our understanding of craft concepts you've already learned, but also discard some of them and write poetry under other kinds of rules—or, sometimes, no rules at all. "Art is disciplined abandon," someone said once, referring to an apparent contradiction: Creating art means saying something that hasn't been said before—by definition, a departure from the rules— but it's impossible to do so without following certain guidelines about what makes one poem better than another. We'll explore this contradiction in our work together this year.

This volume opens with a deep-end-first exercise meant to really loosen your poetry muscles: You will use the week's **seven days to write four poems, one every other day, on four different subjects**. You can use my prompts or come up with your own subjects. Here, perfection in craft is less the goal than to get your poetry motor going.

We'll move on to sections that focus on familiar subjects in new ways. For instance, those who have used previous volumes of this series will remember exercises devoted to **imagery** and **close description**: Because poets take extra care in the words they use for description—there are fewer words in a poem than in a short story, so they weigh that much more—they consider their material (whether an object, feeling, or moment of experience) very closely.

---

32   Koch, Kenneth and Kate Farrell, eds. *Sleeping on the Wing: An Anthology of Modern Poetry with Essays on Reading and Writing.* (New York: Vintage, 1982), p. 294, 296.

We'll move on to a related section, probably still fresh from the fiction section: **word choice**. Poetry, as just mentioned, takes very special care with its words, worrying over them to a degree not usually seen even in fiction. We'll explore that through three new exercises.

Then we'll continue our work with both **sound** and **nonsense**. Poems gain their magic not only from vivid, close description, but rhythm, too. And poems are not usually "first-this-happened, then-that-happened" kind of stories. Poems do tell stories, but just as often, they aim to create a feeling. No exercise makes that more keenly felt than one that does away with comprehension, leaving...what? You'll have to decide.

In a new section, **we'll look closely at many works by a published poet** in order to develop a feeling for his or her work. We'll take this kind of collaboration further by creating an entire poem out of lines by that poet.

Finally, we'll enlarge our scope. So far, we've been looking at poetry as art. But poetry has served as far more than entertainment. Far more than fiction, it's been used to **address history**; in other words, **poetry is political**. We'll consider what that means and practice it ourselves.

As always, you'll close your study with a **culminating poem** using as much of what you've learned this year as possible.

POETRY

INTRODUCTION

WEEK 1

7 DAYS, 4 SUBJECTS, 4 POEMS

Purpose: To loosen up our poetry muscles by diving into the deep end and writing, writing, writing—without much worry about craft concepts.

A lot of our poetry practice in the previous three volumes has consisted of studying craft concepts and then applying them in our poems. This runs counter to the way most poetry textbooks work. They tend to focus on giving young poets ideas on what to write about, and then setting them loose to do it.

This has never made sense to me. How can you write a poem if you don't know what a poem is? Of course, many of us have a rough idea, and having no guidelines is sometimes useful because it lets our imaginations wander free. But my personal feeling is: You learn the rules, and only then ignore them, if you wish.

But you know a lot of rules already. So, this week we'll follow the lead of those other manuals. We're not going to review craft concepts. We're just going to write. If you remember something about line breaks, stanzas, meter, and word choice, and would like to keep them in mind as you write or revise, feel free to. But it's not required. The rules are in you even if you don't call them up consciously. They've *changed* you as a poet; the way you write a poem from scratch now is nothing like the way you did it when you first started to learn the concepts of poetry.

Those of you picking up this series for the first time will be able to ignore craft concepts for a different reason—you haven't encountered them yet. You may find it interesting to do this exercise twice—once this week and once at the end of the course—and compare the results. If you wish, you may substitute a repeat of this Week 1 assignment for the Week 18 assignment.

Now, to the task at hand:

Your assignment: Write a poem every other day this week. End the week with four complete poems.

Below, find 10 subjects to get you going. Feel free to choose your four from the list or come up with your own.

Before you start writing, take note of the following:

Of course, you can skip two days and try to make it up later, but this exercise works best if you stick to the one-every-other-day-plan. Writing a poem is a tall order; to write four in one week is even taller. Help yourself by taking no more than one day off. (And if you'd like, you can spend your off days revising what you did the day before.)

Sitting down to write a poem almost daily also mimics a writer's practice. A committed writer practices virtually every day, often at the same time. Over time, this practice becomes a kind of religion, as regular and important as eating or sleeping. When a writer sits down to work, he or she enters a dedicated zone. Good ideas may or may not arrive, but it's critical for the writer to show up and await them.

Is it possible for you to devote the same chunk of time each day to this assignment? When do you work best? For me, it's the morning. So, if I were doing this assignment, I would aim to rise by 8 (I'm not a very early riser), be in my chair by 8:30, and work on the day's poem from 8:30 to 10:30, without interruptions. (I might devote the first half hour to reading published poems in order to get into a creative mood.)

Ask your family members to help out, by leaving you alone during whichever hours you choose. Try your best to stay in that chair without interruptions. Of course, some write better by wandering around the room, or outside—that's fine. (The short-story writer Ron Carlson insists that the best writers stay in their chairs—that is, having written a good line, they don't congratulate themselves by taking a break. I think you can leave your chair—what you can't do is start folding laundry or checking the Internet or shooting a quick game of hoops.) If you stick it out, the ideas will come.

Think of it as the mental equivalent of exercise. If you pause, your heart rate will slow and when you re-start, it'll be like starting from the beginning.

You may be hankering for at least a little bit of guidance: for instance, "how long should my poem be?" It can be all of one line—we studied single-line poems in last year's volume—or three pages. The only caveat is this: Don't write a one-line poem simply because you're trying to get the assignment over with. I'd suggest that you aim to spend at least two hours on each poem—so you might as well spend them practicing a longer poem. But if you need a guideline, aim for at least 16 lines.

Your 10 optional subjects follow:

1. A poem about an old grandfather clock, and its significance in a family's life and home
2. A poem about the first thing you thought about this morning
3. A poem about something fantastical, like a mouse who writes poems
4. A poem about a place you've never seen
5. A poem in the form of an address to another person
6. A poem to your future self
7. A poem to your younger self, or a younger sibling
8. A poem about your favorite fruit
9. A poem in which you observe something—an object, a process—closely
10. A poem about the last thing you remember dreaming

CHALLENGE EXERCISES:

1. On at least two occasions, devote an hour on your day off to revising the poem.

2. On at least two occasions, begin your two-hour sit-down with a half-hour spent reading poetry by published poets.

DESCRIPTION

A POEM BUILT AROUND A SINGLE METAPHOR

Purpose: To extend our practice of metaphors.

Metaphors, as we've discussed, compare two things by saying that the first *is* the second. **Similes**, on the other hand, compare two things by saying the first is *like* the second. So, "the sky, with its necklace of stars" is a metaphor. "The stars strung up *like* a necklace" is a simile.

Our practice of metaphors has never gone beyond a single comparison: x is y. This week, however, we'll try to extend a single metaphor throughout an entire poem.

Below, you'll find three poems, each followed by a discussion of how the main metaphor runs for the entirety of the poem.

Fog
by Carl Sandburg
(1916)

The fog comes
on little cat feet.

It sits looking
over harbor and city
on silent haunches
and then moves on.[33]

---

33 Sandburg, Carl. "Fog," in *Chicago Poems*. (New York, NY: Henry Holt, 1916) p. 71.

Analysis:

In this poem, Sandburg, a poet of the early 20th century, compares the fog to a cat. Note the way cat imagery occurs throughout the poem: After we are introduced to the comparison—"the fog comes on little cat feet"—the poem goes on to describe as "it sits looking… on silent haunches." I counted at least four references to the fog in feline terms: "little cat feet," "sits looking," "on silent haunches," and "moves on."

To zoom out: Is the metaphor an effective one? Fog and cats don't exactly share shape. A cat is a concrete creature and fog is rather formless. That said, I thought the metaphor was successful because both share a certain furtive, fluid movement, and a kind of watchfulness—not quite human, but alive.

A Noiseless, Patient Spider
by Walt Whitman
(1871-72)

A noiseless, patient spider,
I mark'd where on a little promontory it stood isolated,
Mark'd how to explore the vacant vast surrounding,
It launch'd forth filament, filament, filament, out of itself,
Ever unreeling them, ever tirelessly speeding them.

And you O my soul where you stand,
Surrounded, detached, in measureless oceans of space,
Ceaselessly musing,
venturing, throwing,
seeking the spheres to
connect them,
Till the bridge you will
need be form'd, till the
ductile anchor hold,
Till the gossamer
thread you fling catch
somewhere, O my soul. [34]

34   Whitman, Walt. "A Noiseless Patient Spider," in *Leaves of Grass*. (New York, NY: J. S. Redfield, 1871-72), p.69.

Analysis:

Whitman, the great 19th century poet, uses spider language directly to describe his soul only once, when he writes, "Till the gossamer thread you fling catch somewhere." (Do you know what "gossamer" means? If not, look it up.) Notably, it happens in the last line of the poem, the one likely to stay in his readers' minds the most.

But the metaphor is made clear by other means. For instance, the symmetry in the **form**—the first five-line stanza describes a spider, the next five-line stanza the poet's soul—suggests it. So does the **content**—the spider and the soul both send "filaments" into the world. Through this, they seek connection to a larger universe; the spider through his web, Whitman's soul through its expression in poetry.

Crossing the Bar
by Alfred, Lord Tennyson
(1889)

Sunset and evening star,
    And one clear call for me!
And may there be no moaning of the bar,
    When I put out to sea,
But such a tide as moving seems asleep,
    Too full for sound and foam,
When that which drew from out the boundless deep
    Turns again home.
Twilight and evening bell,
    And after that the dark!
And may there be no sadness of farewell,
    When I embark;
For tho' from out our bourne of Time and Place
    The flood may bear me far,
I hope to see my Pilot face to face
    When I have crost the bar. [35]

---

35 Lord Tennyson, Alfred. "Crossing the Bar," in *Demeter and Other Poems*. (London & New York: Macmillan & Co., 1889), p. 175.

Analysis:

This is a more complicated example. ("Bar" refers to a strip of sand formed by the tides going back and forth.) There's no explicit comparison here, such as we had in the last two poems: Tennyson never says "I am the ship put out to night," or some such. Instead, from the beginning, he plays with a dual definition for the "I" as both man and boat. In the most literal sense, "when I put out to sea" refers to a boat leaving shore. But after two more stanzas of maritime talk—"tide," "foam," "boundless deep" —it's clear the poet is speaking of himself, or at least a person: "I hope to see my Pilot" —that is, God—"face to face." And so, in the final line, the "crossing of the bar" the poem refers to is both a ship's departure into the "boundless deep" and an individual's passage to the next world.

Note as well the way the alternating line lengths—one longer, one shorter—mimic the waves the poem discusses. Here is **form**—the look of the poem—subtly reinforcing its **content**.

Your assignment: Write a poem that maintains a single metaphor for its duration.

Let's discuss steps.

First, come up with a subject: What will you compare to what? How did Carl Sandburg get the idea to compare the fog to a cat? He may have been watching the fog one day, its wisps curling stealthily, and it may have made him think of a cat's movements. Similarly, Whitman may have been watching a spider weaving its web and thought: that's what a poet does, too, his words a web to ensnare his audience. Or it may have happened the other way; Whitman may have been thinking of the poet's essential task—sending his works out into the world, seeking connection with humanity at large—which put him in mind of a spider's work.

Some comparisons to get your mind going:

1. Life is _____.

2. Friendship is _____.

3. Childhood is _____.

4. The rain is _____.

5. The old junky car is _____.

Once you've settled on the first component of the comparison, you'll want to brainstorm about what it's like. Remember—it doesn't have to be like that other thing in every way; only in some single important way. For instance, lots of people say life is a river, full of bends and obstacles and a movement forward you can't stop, but obviously, life isn't wet all the time (unless you live in the Pacific Northwest, perhaps.) What about friendship? Well, friendship is all about bonds, sort of like Whitman's spider. Ants are known for collaboration, too. So you might ask yourself: Who else works in pairs or groups? Or: Where else do we find connection in life? In wires, in telephones and electronic devices. Or perhaps you'd like to highlight another aspect of friendship, namely the way friends can depend on each other. Then you'll try to imagine who or what in life depends on each other.

You may find it more productive to use, as your first component, something very concrete rather than abstract. Life—one of the most abstract notions there is—could be a like a million things, which is a little overwhelming. But an old junky car conjures very specific associations of endurance, fortitude despite disrepair, perseverance, and emotional attachment. It may remind you of an old, wise person you know, or a beetle trying to climb a flower stalk, slipping down, and going at it again.

Once you've settled on your two components, you'll need to make a list of connections between the two. You may want to divide a piece of notebook paper into two columns, with "life" on one side and "river" on the other, or what have you, and create a list of ways in which the one is like the other.

The final and most challenging preparatory step is to figure out how exactly you'll compare the two components. Will you start by saying "x is y," that is, "life is a river"? Or will you use Carl Sandburg's approach: "Life slithers on, a river's belly..." Or perhaps Alfred, Lord Tennyson's, that is, without explicit reference to one of the two components: "It takes the bends and splits the stones with an emptied mind."

Finally, you'll want to think about what you'll be saying in the poem. That is, will you aim solely to compare the two components, or will all this lead to some larger conclusion? Sandburg's poem does not; he merely describes the fog as a cat. Whitman and

Tennyson do more than describe—they link the spider to a soul, and a ship to the self, respectively, but they do so through form rather than content. Whitman never says "the soul is like a spider" and Tennyson never says "I am a ship." Rather, Whitman makes his message clear by lining up the spider stanza and human-soul stanza next to each other; and Tennyson does it, also implicitly, by writing about something so stark, elemental, even epic—a ship setting off into the night—that we can't help making larger conclusions (helped along by his decision, in the last stanza, the one that will stay with the reader the most, to refer to the poet's "Pilot," or God.)

Your turn.

CHALLENGE EXERCISES:

1. Re-write your poem in the styles of Sandburg, Whitman, and Tennyson: That is, as pure description; as two stanzas in which one describes the first component, and the second, the second; and as a poem which ostensibly describes only one thing—a ship, or, in your case, say, the river—but in language that makes clear something larger is being discussed.

2. A later exercise this year will ask you to study closely many works by the same poet. Which poet will be up to you, so unless you have a favorite you know you'd like to focus on, keep an eye out for candidates as you encounter published poems throughout this volume. If either Sandburg, Whitman, or Tennyson caught your eye, you might read another handful of poems by one or each, easy to find on the Internet or in the library. (A great site for poetry is **poets.org**, the official site of the Academy of American Poets.) Wikipedia, meanwhile, can offer a handy introduction to their lives.

CLOSE DESCRIPTION OF AN OBJECT

Purpose: To focus our descriptive powers repeatedly on a single item throughout a poem.

In earlier volumes of this series, you practiced close observation and description of objects. Let's see how good you've gotten.

As you did last week, start by reading the published poem below. A quick analysis follows it. Just as Emily Dickinson focuses on balloons, your mission this week will be to describe something—an object, a feeling, a thought, a vision—closely for the duration of a whole poem.

The Balloon
by Emily Dickinson
(1863)

You've seen balloons set, haven't you?
So stately they ascend
It is as swans discarded you
For duties diamond.

Their liquid feet go softly out
Upon a sea of blond;
They spurn the air as 't were too mean
For creatures so renowned.

Their ribbons just beyond the eye,
They struggle some for breath,
And yet the crowd applauds below;
They would not encore death.

The gilded creature strains and spins,
Trips frantic in a tree,
Tears open her imperial veins
And tumbles in the sea.

The crowd retire with an oath
The dust in streets goes down,
And clerks in counting-rooms observe,
"'T was only a balloon."[36]

Analysis:

A cheeky little poem by Emily Dickinson about hot-air balloons. And yet, it shows us how much beauty can be wrung out of an ordinary object if we just look closely enough. Look at Dickinson's majestic descriptions of the balloon: In the first stanza, she compares it to a swan; in the second, she treats it as a living object, walking its "liquid feet" over the air, then "spurn[ing]" the air as not good enough to house its royal ascent. The balloon continues as a living object in the third and fourth stanzas— "struggle some for breath," "tears open her imperial veins." The fifth pivots from a concentration on the balloon to something much broader: how quickly human wonder—at the balloon, in this case—turns to diminishment of the object in question. Just a moment ago, the crowd was singing the balloon's wonders; now it's trying to write it off as no big thing.

Your assignment: Devote a poem to close, repeated description of a single object. What object is up to you.

How to choose a subject? One idea is to spend a day noting what catches your attention. If you find yourself having more than a passing thought about something—two

36 Dickinson, Emily. *Poems by Emily Dickinson, Third Series.* (Boston: Little, Brown, 1906), p. 128.

deer chewing grass in the woods, the shimmer of sun on a lake, the rumble of a tractor engine—flag it.

Once you've settled on the subject, you'll want to decide what exactly you're going to say about it. Will you describe its functions, as Emily Dickinson does in her poem? Or its significance in the world you inhabit? Or the feelings it elicits? Or will you use it to make some larger point about human beings, or the way life goes, as Dickinson also does? Whichever path you choose, your primary mission is to find new ways to describe the object as the poem goes on.

Before you start writing, you can draw up a list of its qualities. If we're talking about a tractor, ask yourself:

What does it look like?

What does it sound like?

What does it do?

What are things like without it?

How does it smell?

Who uses it?

What is this person like?

What does it make you think of?

When do you see it?

Try to answer each of these questions in as much detail as possible. After you've answered them literally—"the tractor is red, with green trim and large black tires"—try to extend the description into metaphor or simile: "The tractor plods forth like a horse." From that, you might jump into a variation on what we did last week: using the language of a horse to describe the tractor: "The tractor whinnies out of its sleeping-shed, the great hooded eyes lazy in the morning light."

After you've brainstormed about the immediate descriptive details, you can think about whether you'd like to make a larger point about it. Perhaps you'd like to note that a tractor is the unsung hero of a farm. Or maybe you want to present the tractor's field work not as the highlight of its day, but as a mere preamble to its return to the tractor shed, where, after the lights go down, it has a separate, living existence together with the other items—thresher, spades, pickaxes—that live there.

As in the past, if you're not sure how many lines your poem should have, aim for 16. If a natural rhythm doesn't recommend itself, you could copy Emily Dickinson's approach: or regular stanzas of four lines apiece, in Dickinson's.

CHALLENGE EXERCISE:

In a tribute to Emily Dickinson's devotion of so much majestic description to a hot-air balloon, pick the most unremarkable object you can find—a discarded sock, a toaster, the pen you're writing with. Do this exercise about *that* object, trying to find the special in the ordinary.

But you don't have to be so solemn about it—an earnest, grave poem about a discarded sock might sound silly and self-important. You could write a *comic* poem about the discarded sock, exaggerating its importance as a way of showing its actual lack of significance, or treating it as a living object and writing a poem from its perspective, tracing its path from drawer to your foot, to the laundry hamper, to the wash, and back into your drawer. The bottom line here is that even the simplest objects have vivid lives if you just pause and think about it.

POETRY · SECTION 2

WORD CHOICE AND REVISION

WEEKS 4 - 6

TWO TRANSLATIONS

Purpose: To see how different translators have translated the same poem, as a window into word choice.

In previous levels of this course, you've practiced choosing words carefully, often by brainstorming various ways to say the same thing. We'll practice the same skill this week, but using a different approach. We'll look at three translations of the same poem (originally in a foreign language), in order to understand how differently the same material can be rendered in English. The greater point is to understand how many different words can say the same thing.

One of the most striking examples of how differently the same lines can be translated into English comes from the great Russian poet Alexander Pushkin's novel-in-verse *Eugene Onegin*. Pushkin is notoriously hard to translate, partly for the obvious reason that poetry in a foreign language will always lose something in translation. But Pushkin is especially difficult because he wrote beautiful, musical poetry, strictly rhymed and heavily metered, in the original Russian. To get his poetry into English while preserving the meter *and* the sing-song sound is a tall challenge, indeed.

Many have tried. The difficulty of the effort led at least one translator—Vladimir Nabokov, a native Russian speaker, and better-known as one of the great novelists of the 20th century—to say: I'm not even going to try to capture the meter. Nabokov translated *Onegin* literally—that is, paying greater attention to the accurate translation of Russian words into English than to preservation of the original's rhythm. *We'll lose the sing-song*, Nabokov's message seems to be, *but we'll get the meaning exactly as Pushkin intended it.* Most others have chosen to preserve the music of the original, instead sacrificing perfect fidelity to the meaning of the original.

We don't have to get into the question of whose approach is more sensible. Each side has its supporters; in fact, how to get across both the letter and the spirit of an original is one of the most enduring challenges of translation. Our goal this week is less to evaluate the quality of these translations than to use them for our purposes: to observe how the same thing can be said in vastly different ways.

Below, I present the first stanza of the first chapter in the original Russian. I assume you don't speak it, but it may be interesting to see what Russian looks like, and at the very least, you'll get to see the shape of the lines and the poem as a whole.

After that, you'll find three translations, one by Henry Spalding from 1881, one by Walter Arndt from 1963 (the one Nabokov was responding to with his translation), and then the literal one by Nabokov from 1964. The inclusion of the Spalding is meant to show you how English **diction**—choice of vocabulary, style of expression—has changed in the last century-plus. Your assignment this week will be to join the illustrious list of *Onegin* translators. You'll try your hand at a "translation" of the stanza—not from the Russian, but using the other three translations as a basis to put the lines into your own words.

Here is Pushkin's original Russian:

Мой дядя самых честных правил,
Когда не в шутку занемог,
Он уважать себя заставил
И лучше выдумать не мог.
Его пример другим наука;
Но, боже мой, какая скука
С больным сидеть и день и ночь,
Не отходя ни шагу прочь!
Какое низкое коварство
Полуживого забавлять,
Ему подушки поправлять,
Печально подносить лекарство,
Вздыхать и думать про себя:
Когда же черт возьмет тебя!

Now read the following three translations, which I've arranged from the most recent (Nabokov) to the oldest.

Nabokov (1964)

"My uncle has most honest principles:
when taken ill in earnest,
he has made one respect him
and nothing better could invent.
To others his example is a lesson;
but, good God, what a bore
to stick by a sick man both day and night,
without moving a step away!
What base perfidiousness
the half-alive one to amuse,
adjust for him the pillows,
sadly present the medicine,
sigh—and think inwardly
when *will* the devil take you?"[37]

Walter Arndt (1963)

"Now that he is in grave condition,
My uncle, decorous old dunce,
Has won respectful recognition;
And done the perfect thing for once.
His action be a guide to others;
But what a bore, I ask you, brothers,
To tend a patient night and day
And venture not a step away:
Is there hypocrisy more glaring
Than to amuse one all but dead,
Shake up the pillow for his head,
Dose him with melancholy bearing,

---

37 Pushkin, Alexander. *Eugene Onegin*. Trans. Vladimir Nabokov. New York: Pantheon, 1964.

And think behind a public sigh:
'Deuce take you, step on it and die!'" [38]

Henry Spalding (1881)

"My uncle's goodness is extreme,
If seriously he hath disease;
He hath acquired the world's esteem
And nothing more important sees;
A paragon of virtue he!
But what a nuisance it will be,
Chained to his bedside night and day
Without a chance to slip away.
Ye need dissimulation base
A dying man with art to soothe,
Beneath his head the pillow smooth,
And physic bring with mournful face,
To sigh and meditate alone:
When will the devil take his own!" [39]

Your assignment: "Translate" the stanza into your own words, line by line.

Start out by using the Nabokov translation to get a sense of what the stanza is saying—the narrator's lament about having to tend to an uncle who has fallen ill. As you read the others, start to summarize as succinctly as possible what's going in individual lines. You'll want to end up with thumbnails for each of the stanza's 14 lines. That will serve as your guideline when you re-translate the stanza.

Then, flesh out each line, choosing your own words to convey the meanings. Take care to avoid leaning too much on the words chosen by the other translators. Of course, there's only one way to say certain things—"uncle," "pillows"—but when dealing with those words or phrases that clearly required choosing ("matchless," "man of honour," "acted very wisely"), try to pick your own original phrasing.

38 Pushkin, Alexander. *Eugene Onegin.* Trans. Walter Arndt. New York N.Y.: The Overlook Press, 2002.
39 Pushkin, Alexander. *Eugene Onegin.* Trans. Henry Spalding. London: Macmillan and Co., 1881.

CHALLENGE EXERCISE:

1. How well can you do with a single sentence? Albert Camus' *The Stranger* has had many a translator. Here are just some of the different ways in which the first lines have been rendered:

The French original (1942): "Aujourd'hui, maman est morte. Ou peut-être hier, je ne sais pas. J'ai reçu un télégramme de l'asile: Mère décédée. Enterrement demain. Sentiments distingués. Cela ne veut rien dire. C'était peut-être hier." [40]

Stuart Gilbert (1946): "Mother died today. Or, maybe, yesterday; I can't be sure. The telegram from the Home says: Your mother passed away. Funeral tomorrow. Deep sympathy. Which leaves the matter doubtful; it could have been yesterday." [41]

Joseph Laredo (1982): "Mother died today. Or maybe yesterday, I don't know. I had a telegram from the home: 'Mother passed away. Funeral tomorrow. Yours sincerely.' That doesn't mean anything. It may have been yesterday." [42]

Matthew Ward (1988): "Maman died today. Or yesterday maybe, I don't know. I got a telegram from the home: Mother deceased. Funeral tomorrow. Faithfully yours. That doesn't mean anything. Maybe it was yesterday." [43]

Before you try your own hand at the line, how do the versions differ? What different feelings do they inspire?

2. In 1987, the Mexican poet Octavio Paz and his English-language translator Eliot Weinberger published a book called *19 Ways of Looking at Wang Wei: How a Chinese Poem is Translated*, which featured 19 wildly different translations of the poem in question. Look it up in your local library.

---

40 Camus, Albert. *L'Etranger*. Paris: Librairie Gallimard, 1942.
41 Camus, Albert. *The Plague*. Trans. Stuart Gilbert. (New York, NY: A.A. Knopf, 1948.)
42 Camus, Albert. *The Plague*. Trans. Joseph Laredo. (London: Hamish Hamilton, 1982.)
43 Camus, Albert. *The Plague*. Trans. Matthew Ward. (New York, NY: Random House, 1988.)

3. The website Readwritethink.org, which features tons of resources for anyone interested in poetry, includes not only five translations of an excerpt from the epic poem *Beowulf*, but some introductory information about this poem as well. Find it here: http://www.readwritethink.org/files/resources/interactives/beowulf/.

4. If you happen to speak a foreign language, even better: using a search engine on the Web, find a poet who's written in that language and has had his work translated by at least two different people. This kind of repeated translation is usually reserved for the best-known foreign poets, so it shouldn't be too hard to find someone. Then do a third translation with the benefit of your understanding of the original.

5. In the library, look up the July 11, 1994 issue of *The New Yorker*. It features a profile of the painter David Salle by the journalist Janet Malcolm called "Forty-One False Starts." Malcolm couldn't figure out how to start her article about Salle, chucking version after version. So she made *that*—her 41 false starts—the profile. It's an incredible example of how to approach the same subject from different directions.

A SELF-CREATED WORKSHOP

Purpose: To get feedback from a variety of readers on a poem you've written.

Last week, we looked at a series of translations, examining how many different ways the same thing can be said. Next week, you'll "re-translate"—in other words, revise—one of your own poems (over and over).

To prepare for next week's assignment, you'll need to get some ideas about how you might best rework your poem.

One of the great benefits of a college creative writing course, or a post-college Master's in Fine Arts program, is that you can "work-shop" your poems and stories—give them to other readers and listen to their feedback. You get the benefit of a dozen pairs of additional eyes on your work. This doesn't come without its own problems—some readers may not be good judges of poetry, and their opinions will have to be ignored. But sometimes, a careful, well-matched reader can help you understand your own poem in new ways.

So, this week you are going to create for yourself a facsimile of a creative writing work-shop. You will find five people with whom to share a poem you've written in order to get their "feedback." I know you may be hesitant to share your poetry with anyone but your mentor, but I would encourage you to try to overcome that. Poetry doesn't have to be a public endeavor—that is, it doesn't have to be written for a public audience—but it can be an amazing tool of connection. Chances are the things you're writing about are things that have occurred to others, and to encounter them in written form can be a great fulfillment for readers. In this way, poetry can build bridges between people. In short, poetry can build community.

Poetry can teach readers, too—new ways of seeing, new ways of thinking, new ways of saying things. So I'd like you to try to imagine that your poem will be a delight to those whom you give it to, that they will be honored to have a look and be asked to provide suggestions. In turn, you have to understand their feedback and recommendations as the suggestions of readers likely to have a great deal of faith in your work—not the criticism of people who think you have no talent.

But that's secondary. The primary goal this week is to get ideas on how to re-work your poem: Whether something should be cut, something else added, a third thing moved, a fourth re-phrased. Perhaps someone in your circle of contacts is particular about words and can suggest a more vivid alternative to "scared," such as "spooked." Maybe someone else won't be able to propose an improvement, but will flag a line that doesn't make sense, or could be clearer. And so forth.

Obviously, you should pick people you trust—your mentor, a sibling, a friend. Remind them that they don't have to be poetry experts in order to give you feedback. The poem wasn't written for the experts, was it? But if they would like some guidance on how to respond, you could ask them to answer some of these questions:

What is the poem about?

What about it do you think works well, and what doesn't?

If you were writing it, what would you change?

Pick three words that you think could be improved.

Pick three sentences or sentence fragments that could be phrased more clearly or more elegantly.

Do you think everything is where it should be, or would you move some things around?

Would you cut anything? Add anything?

Would you make it longer? Shorter?

What does it make you think of?

What does it make you feel?

You can ask your participants to write out the answers. This may also help in avoiding the occasional difficulty of being "criticized" to one's face—and of having to give criticism, however constructive, directly to another's.

Your assignment: Choose one of your own original poems. Share it with five readers. Ask them to give you feedback about what works and what doesn't. If they don't seem able to come up with concrete suggestions, or if they ask you for directions, give them the list of questions above.

Then, spend some time thinking about the feedback from your five workshop members and making notes in your notebook (at least one page) about what you might re-work in your poem next week.

CHALLENGE EXERCISE:

Does anyone else you know write poetry? Contact them to see if, for one week, they'd like to participate in an actual workshop. As little as three participants can make for a great one. The three of you would circulate your poems to each other and then meet for 2 hours at some point to share feedback, devoting 30-40 minutes to each poem.

7 DAYS, 1 SUBJECT, 4 REVISIONS

Purpose: To re-translate our own poems several times.

This week, you'll be bringing the lessons of the last two weeks to their culmination: You'll be "re-translating" your own poem several times based on the feedback you received last week from your "self-created workshop."

This week also borrows in spirit from the exercise that opened the poetry section of this volume: A new task every other day of the week.

Think of one of the revisions as simply a "re-translation." Approach it as a kind of game, aiming to re-write the same lines in a new way (without changing anything else).

But surely last week's critiques brought forth other ideas on how you might improve your poem: Ideas having to do with all the other aspects of poetry that we've studied through this series and this year. To refresh our discussion from last week, things you can do include:

- Re-phrasing some of the words and expressions

- Re-organizing lines or even stanzas

- Cutting certain things, adding others

- Playing with the line lengths and how many lines you have in your stanzas

- Approaching the poem from the perspective of sound: Does it use sound in an interesting way? Do any sounds crop up frequently, or perhaps should, depending on what you're writing about? Does the poem "sound" like what you're writing about (e.g., is it full of hard consonants [k, t, d] if you're describing something tough, or vowels and soft consonants [s, w, v, l] if not?)?

- Are you describing as vividly as you can? Thinking about something as closely as you can?

- How are your comparisons? Perhaps they can be stronger or more precise?

- Are there any clichés? You'll want to wipe those out.

The value of revision:

As I've mentioned, the first draft that pours out of us is almost never our best: we're groping in the dark, trying to figure out how to translate from our brains onto the page. In the second draft—and third, and fourth, and so on—you ask yourself to think more closely and deeply about your poem. If you don't believe that a second draft will make a better poem, give it a shot. I revised my novel—changing a substantial number of its 100,000 words every time—a dozen times. It got better with each its variation. As the poet Donald Hall has explained: "You should stare at a poem long enough so that you have one hundred reasons for using every comma, one hundred reasons for every linebreak, one hundred reasons for every *and* and *or*… Spontaneity is no virtue. Spontaneity tells lies that deliberate, careful thought can alter into truth." [44]

I've also discussed the value of revising over and over—Donald Hall sometimes revises 600 times—but I've usually counseled you to take a break between versions, so that your mind has a chance to rest and you can approach each draft with fresh eyes. That's the reason I'm asking you for four revisions this week rather than seven—one on the

44 Lammon, Martin. "Flying Revision's Flag." Interview with Donald Hall. Originally published in *Kestral* in 1993. Reprinted in Donald Hall, *Death to the Death of Poetry* (Ann Arbor, MI: University of Michigan Press, 1994) pg. 92.

first day, one on the third, one on the fifth, and one on the seventh. But I *am* assigning such a rapid-fire set of revisions 1) in order to provide a crash course in revision and 2) to demonstrate, in a compressed time frame, the value of going at something again and again. First of all, thinking so deeply about the same poem over and over—kind of like daily football practice, or ballet, or anything—changes your relationship to it from something you do casually to something you do as a regular practice. Also, it allows you to see results quickly: I guarantee your poem on Day 7 will be four times better than the one from Day 1.

Before I leave you to the task, let's have a quick look at what revision looks like for a published poet. Elizabeth Bishop, one of the greatest poets of the 20th century, revised endlessly, down to the individual word, as all poets should. Take the first line of her poem "The Bight" (1948-49): "At low tide like this how sheer the water is." At first, Bishop considered:

> At low tide like
> this how sheer the water is.

Then:

> At low tide
> like this
> how sheer
> the water is.

Then:

> At low tide like this how sheer
> the water is.

And, finally:

> At low tide like this how sheer the water is.

Any ideas why she settled on this version?

The site Writersdigest.com, where I first encountered this example, says that Bishop didn't specify except to say that the "long, almost elastic single line coincided with the mood of the speaker in the poem. Those words needed breadth, perhaps, as in a deep inhalation and then exhalation on the reader's part."

Another guess might be just as good. There's an obvious echo between "this" and "is," but a breakdown like this—

> At low tide like this
> How sheer the water is.

—seemed a little simplistic, perhaps. Note as well the sound relationships of the line: The patter of the "l"s and "t"s in the first half ("*low tide like this*") and the exchange of the "r"s and "w"s in the second ("ho*w* she*er* the *w*ate*r*"). Bishop may have wanted the symmetry of those echoes in one rapid line; once again, splitting them up into two neat lines may have been just that: too neat.

All of this is rational conjecture on my part—chances are Bishop chose what she did based on instinct alone. The line she ended up using "felt" right, for reasons she herself may not have been able to explain. After enough practice, you'll develop a similar intuition. Until then, just give it your best shot. For now, make sure to register the most important thing: How much attention and effort the famous poet put into figuring out a single line.

Your assignment: Revise your chosen poem four times this week, giving one day's rest between each revision. On the first day, simply, "re-translate" your poem without making other changes. On the third, fifth, and seventh days, rework the poem more substantially. You can do that in several different ways. Or you can revise on the third day, rework your revision on the fifth, and re-edit your reworked revision on the seventh. The choice is up to you. But you should end up with four different versions of your original poem.

At week's end, pick your favorite version. Then ask your mentor to pick *his or her* favorite. Did you choose the same one?

CHALLENGE EXERCISES:

1. Look up "The Bight" by Elizabeth Bishop in its entirety online. Does the rest of the poem shed any light on why she settled on the version of the first line that she did?

2. In the library, find and flip through *Poem, Revised: 54 Poems, Revisions, Discussions*, edited by Robert Hartwell Fiske and Laura Cherry. (Marion Street Press, 2008.)

3. On the Poets.org website, read the entirety of Martin Lammon's conversation with Donald Hall about the value of revision: http://www.poets.org/viewmedia.php/prmMID/16223.

POETRY • SECTION 3

SOUND

WEEKS 7 - 9

RECITATION

Purpose: To appreciate a poem's sound through oral recitation.

This week, we'll study a poem's sound through a new tool: Memorization and recitation. After discussing its value, I present several poems that make for especially fun memorization.

As you may know, neither fiction nor poetry started out on the page. They started orally, as stories told around fires in ancient times. To make these stories and poems easier to remember, their creators filled them with repetition—of events, of turns of phrase, and especially in the case of poetry, of sounds. So, to this day, oral recitation of poetry remains not only a great way to connect to the origins of poetry, but to experience the sound of a poem in a whole new way.

Your assignment this week will have three parts, culminating in the memorization and oral recitation of a poem to your mentor (or anyone else who will listen).

Your assignment, Part 1: Below you will find three poems. Start out by reading each poem aloud twice.

Remember what we've discussed about reading out loud:

Begin by reading each poem silently to yourself.

Pause at commas, periods, line breaks, and stanza breaks, in order of increasing length. You should be pausing at a stanza break longer than seems natural in ordinary speech. Figure it like this: Comma (.5 seconds), period (1 second), line break (1 second), stanza (2 seconds). Of course, stanzas that end on an unfinished sentence make this harder—just do your best.

After reading the poem aloud, do it again, this time focusing less on getting the words right than on noticing how differently it sounds out loud compared to on the page. Try to note, as well, how your own experience of the poem changed. This might be a great thing to discuss with your mentor. Having an interlocutor will help tease out your feelings on the matter.

1.

The Lake Isle of Innisfree
by William Butler Yeats
(1890)

I will arise and go now, and go to Innisfree,
And a small cabin build there, of clay and wattles made:
Nine bean-rows will I have there, a hive for the honey-bee;
And live alone in the bee-loud glade.

And I shall have some peace there, for peace comes dropping slow,
Dropping from the veils of the morning to where the cricket sings;
There midnight's all a glimmer, and noon a purple glow,
And evening full of the linnet's wings.

I will arise and go now, for always night and day
I hear lake water lapping with low sounds by the shore;
While I stand on the roadway, or on the pavements grey,
I hear it in the deep heart's core.[45]

---

45 William Butler Yeats. "Lake Isle of Innisfree," *Countess Kathleen and Other Legends and Lyrics* (Boston: Roberts Bros., 1892).

2.

Jabberwocky
by Lewis Carroll
(1871)

'Twas brillig, and the slithy toves
    Did gyre and gimble in the wabe:
All mimsy were the borogoves,
    And the mome raths outgrabe.

"Beware the Jabberwock, my son!
    The jaws that bite, the claws that catch!
Beware the Jubjub bird, and shun
    The frumious Bandersnatch!"

He took his vorpal sword in hand;
    Long time the manxome foe he sought—
So rested he by the Tumtum tree
    And stood awhile in thought.

And, as in uffish thought he stood,
    The Jabberwock, with eyes of flame,
Came whiffling through the tulgey wood,
    And burbled as it came!

One, two! One, two! And through and through
    The vorpal blade went snicker-snack!
He left it dead, and with its head
    He went galumphing back.

"And hast thou slain the Jabberwock?
    Come to my arms, my beamish boy!
O frabjous day! Callooh! Callay!"
    He chortled in his joy.

'Twas brillig, and the slithy toves
    Did gyre and gimble in the wabe:

All mimsy were the borogoves,
　　And the mome raths outgrabe.[46]

3.　　　　　　　**Beat! Beat! Drums!**

by Walt Whitman
(1861)

Beat! beat! drums!—blow! bugles! blow!

Through the windows—through doors—burst like a ruthless force,

Into the solemn church, and scatter the congregation,

Into the school where the scholar is studying,

Leave not the bridegroom quiet—no happiness must he have now with his bride,

Nor the peaceful farmer any peace, ploughing his field or gathering his grain,

So fierce you whirr and pound you drums—so shrill you bugles blow.

Beat! beat! drums!—blow! bugles! blow!

Over the traffic of cities—over the rumble of wheels in the streets;

Are beds prepared for sleepers at night in the houses? no sleepers must sleep in
　　those beds,

No bargainers' bargains by day—no brokers or speculators—would they continue?

Would the talkers be talking? would the singer attempt to sing?

Would the lawyer rise in the court to state his case before the judge?

Then rattle quicker, heavier drums—you bugles wilder blow.

Beat! beat! drums!—blow! bugles! blow!

Make no parley—stop for no expostulation,

Mind not the timid—mind not the weeper or prayer,

Mind not the old man beseeching the young man,

Let not the child's voice be heard, nor the mother's entreaties,

Make even the trestles to shake the dead where they lie awaiting the hearses,

So strong you thump, O terrible drums—so loud you bugles blow.[47]

---

46 Lewis Carroll. *Through the Looking-Glass (And What Alice Found There)*. (London: Macmillan & Co., 1871).

47 Walt Whitman. "Beat! Beat! Drums!" *Leaves of Grass*. (Philadelphia: David McKay, 1891-92).

Your assignment, Part 2: Memorize one of the poems above. Choose your favorite. Go to YouTube and see if you can find other oral recitations. Listen to how those readers treat the rhythms and meters, the rhymes and repeated sounds. Then, commit your chosen poem to memory.

Your assignment, Part 3: Perform your memorized poem for your mentor—and anyone else who will listen.

CHALLENGE EXERCISES:

1. Read several more poems by one of the three poets mentioned. A search online will bring you to many options.

2. Go further with memorization. *Committed to Memory: 100 Best Poems to Memorize,* edited by John Hollander (Books & Co. 1996) will give you many examples. A digest of the book is available here: https://www.poets.org/viewmedia.php/prmMID/17111.

3. Mark out a rhyme scheme, if one exists, for each of the three poems in the exercise.

Quick refresher: Any lines that end in the same or a similar sound are marked by the same letter, such as A. The next new sound gets a B, and so forth. For example, the first two stanzas of W. B. Yeats' poem are: ABAB.

4. Using one of the poems as a model, write a brief poem of your own (it can have as many lines as your model poem) that stresses sound through the kind of patterning you saw in the lesson. For instance, if the dominant element is rhyme, you can emphasize that; if it's alliteration, that; if repetition of words or phrases, that; and so forth.

RHYME AND METER IN POPULAR SONG

Purpose: To learn about sound through another form.

Unfortunately, poetry sometimes gets locked up in the attic. That is, it's both taught as—and misunderstood to be—some kind of dusty, academic relic. But poetry is as alive, and as relevant to our daily lives, as we allow it to be. Poetry is people trying to express something about the lives we all lead.

So it shouldn't surprise you that poetry shares a great deal with other art forms, such as pop music. The missions of poetry and pop are almost identical: To write words and beats so catchy that you won't be able to stop listening.

This week's lesson is a reminder of this affinity. We'll look at a fragment of the lyrics to a song by Faithless, a British band. It's full of quite inventive rhyme (both **end rhyme** and **internal rhyme**), as well as **meter**. You'll remember meter as the counting of syllables and accents in poetry. Didn't think that could be done to a song as well? I'm sure the songwriters of Faithless didn't plot out their lyrics with meter in mind, but they're such experienced musicians that they chose the words with consistent, singable meter. There are only so many syllables you can cram into a single breath without rushing or stretching the sound.

This week's assignment has two parts. In the first, we'll treat the lyrics to the song (as rendered on Faithless' official website) as a written poem. We'll determine the rhyme scheme, count out syllables, and mark where the stress falls when we say the lines out loud.

In the second part of the exercise, we'll look at the same lines in a very different way: as an oral document, something meant to be spoken out loud rather than read. It will be interesting for you to compare the sound of the lines as you imagined it with their performance by Maxi Jazz, the Faithless vocalist. Poetry is as alive as a biological organism. Emphasize certain syllables and it reads one way; emphasize others, and it reads another. Maxi Jazz chooses to perform the lines one way—but that's not the only option.

Your assignment, Part 1:

1. Below, you'll find the first 20 lines from the song "Bring My Family Back" by Faithless. Read them to yourself. Read them out loud. Then ask your mentor to read them to you.

2. Do a rhyme scheme for the 20 lines. That is, find each sound that rhymes with another sound. (Within reason: The word "three" in Line 1 rhymes with the word "we" in Line 7, but that's not what I'm talking about; I mean rhymes close to each other.) Mark every similar sound with the same letter of the alphabet. The next set of similar sounds gets the next letter of the alphabet and so forth. Pay special attention to **internal rhyme**: rhyming words that don't appear at the ends of the lines. When you're finished, examine your work. Is there a regular rhyme scheme?

3. Divide up every line into syllables, such as:

I'm on lone-ly street age near-ly three

Re-cent-ly Ma-ma's cry-ing all the time[48]

You'll find my own answers for #2 and #3 below. Please don't look at them until you've tried your own hand at the rhyme scheme and syllable count.

---

48 Dictionary.com can help you find out how to divide words into syllables. For a more general lesson on the rules of breaking words into syllables, check out: http://www.howmanysyllables. com/howtocountsyllables.html

Here are the opening 20 lines of the song, numbered.

1. "Bring My Family Back"

1   I'm on lonely street age nearly three
2   Recently Mama's crying all the time
3   is it because of me or my younger sister,
4   even Dad was weeping when he kissed her.
5   Face all puffy like a blister,
6   crying like he missed her.
7   Since we moved away from the house,
8   where we used to play.
9   They say I'll understand one day but I doubt it,
10 Mama never say nothing about it.
11 How'd it get to be so crowded.
12 I found it a strain, everywhere I look I see pain.
13 And I can't escape the feeling,

14 maybe I'm to blame. So I strain to listen,

15 Praying for a decision, wishing they were kissing.

16 This feels like extradition or exile,

17 Mama finds it hard to smile

18 So I make pretend cups of coffee in her favorite style.

19 She says child I'm working so there's nothing you lack.

20 But she know I want my Dad I want my family back.[49]

Here are my answers...

2. Rhyme scheme

1 I'm on lonely street age nearly **three [A]**

2 Recent**ly [A]** Mama's crying all the time

3 is it because of **me [A]** or my younger **sister, [B]**

4 even Dad was weeping when he **kissed her. [B]**

5 Face all puffy like a **blister, [B]**

6 crying like he **missed her. [B]**

7 Since we moved away from the house,

8 where we used to **play. [C]**

9 They say I'll understand one **day [C]** but I **doubt it, [D]**

10 Mama never say nothing **about it. [D]**

11 **How'd it [D]** get to be so **crowded. [D]**

12 I found **it [D]** a **strain, [E]** everywhere I look I see **pain. [E]**

13 And I can't escape the feeling,

14 maybe I'm to **blame. [E]** So I **strain [E]** to **listen, [F]**

15 Praying for a **decision, [F] wishing [F]** they were **kissing. [F]**

16 This feels like **extradition [F]** or **exile, [G]**

17 Mama finds it hard to **smile [G]**

18 So I make pretend cups of coffee in her favorite **style. [G]**

19 She says **child [G]** I'm working so there's nothing you **lack. [H]**

20 But she know I want my Dad I want my family **back. [H]**

49   "Bring My Family Back," from *Sunday 8PM*, by Faithless/Max Frasier/Rollo Armstrong/Ayalah
    Bentovim, Cheeky Records/BMG (1998)

Is there a rhyme scheme?

The song has no strict rhyme scheme, but several patterns emerge. Let's track the rhymes as the opening stanza proceeds:

- A is an end rhyme followed by two internal rhymes
- B is four end rhymes
- C, D, E, and F work roughly as A does
- G has one internal rhyme but looks more like B
- H is all end rhymes, which made me think of a sonnet, whose final two lines share a distinct rhyme. So you can think of this 20-line stanza as a very loose, modern variation on the stanza: 18 lines with 7 rhyme schemes (and, just as importantly, three lines without any end rhymes) and then a closing **couplet**.
- One of my favorite parts of the lyrics is its use of **internal rhymes**, and the way they serve as a transition from one rhyme sound to another. That is a nearly constant aspect of the stanza.

What did *you* think of the rhyme scheme?

3. Syllable count

1 I'm on lone-ly street age near-ly three **[9 syllables]**
2 Re-cent-ly Ma-ma's cry-ing all the time **[10]**
3 is it be-cause of me or my young-er sis-ter, **[12]**
4 e-ven Dad was weep-ing when he kissed her. **[10]**
5 Face all puff-y like a blis-ter, **[8]**
6 cry-ing like he missed her. **[6]**
7 Since we moved a-way from the house, **[8]**
8 where we used to play. **[5]**
9 They say I'll un-der-stand one day but I doubt it, **[12]**
10 Ma-ma nev-er say noth-ing a-bout it. **[10]**
11 How'd it get to be so crowd-ed. **[8]**
12 I found it a strain, eve-ry-where I look I see pain. **[13]**
13 And I can't es-cape the feel-ing, **[8]**
14 may-be I'm to blame. So I strain to lis-ten, **[11]**
15 Pray-ing for a de-ci-sion, wish-ing they were kiss-ing. **[13]**
16 This feels like ex-tra-di-tion or ex-ile, **[10]**
17 Ma-ma finds it hard to smile **[7]**

18 So I make pre-tend cups of cof-fee in her fa-vor-ite style. **[15]**
19 She says child I'm work-ing so there's noth-ing you lack. **[12]**
20 But she know I want my Dad I want my fam-i-ly back. **[14]**

The syllable count is as inconsistent as the rhyme scheme, if we're being strict. But evaluated more loosely, it typically hovers somewhere around the 10-syllable mark, which, as you may remember from a lesson last year, is the size of a human breath.

Now for the last and trickiest part of this assignment:

4. Try to **scan** the 20 lines: that is, bold those syllables that seem to get emphasized when you say the words out loud.

I'll do the first five lines for you. You're on your own for the rest.

A quick meter refresher:

As we discussed in last year's volume, the default for the lines we write is what's known as **iambic pentameter**: An iamb is a two-syllable unit where the first syllable is unemphasized and the second is emphasized. The human breath lasts for about 10 syllables, or five (penta-) two-syllable units (known as **feet**). So that a line of iambic pentameter reads like this: da-DUM, da-DUM, da-DUM, da-DUM, da-DUM. (Shakespeare: "If **mu**-sic **be** the **food** of **love**, play **on**.") You can mark out the reading of the line by tapping your palm on the table in unison.

1 **I'm** on **lone**-ly **street age near**-ly **three**

Song lyrics hew less closely to these guidelines than poems; this line, for instance, has nine syllables. Also, in the opening syllables, "I'm" seems to matter more than "on."

In the next two-syllable unit (it may help you to tackle scansion in terms of two-syllable units, even if they span more than one word; "lone-ly" is two syllables, but so is "I'm on"), the answer seemed simple: When pronouncing "lone-ly," it's the first syllable that gets the stress.

The next two-syllable unit—"street age" —is a bit of a trick. The song lyric "swallows" some words. A more traditional, narrative line of poetry would follow a word like "street" with a preposition like "that" or "where." (And "street" would be emphasized while the preposition would not be.) But because that word is skipped here, we jump right to another important word ("age"), so I'd emphasize both "street" and "age."

"Near-ly" works more traditionally, just like "lone-ly" did: the first syllable gets emphasized when the word is pronounced out loud.

"Three" can go either way, but I decided to bold it because when I read the line out loud I seemed to emphasize it, though perhaps only because it followed an unstressed syllable ("ly").

One very important note: scansion is fluid. Two people will scan the same written line in two different ways, depending on how they hear it in their minds. So, please don't think of this as an exercise with one single answer. Your job here is merely to get a handle on how these lines might get scanned. Again, they're not traditional lines of poetry, so scanning them is much tougher than scanning something regular by Shakespeare.

2 **Re**-cent-ly **Ma**-ma's **cry**-ing **all** the **time**

In the previous line, we measured the syllables in units of two. With this line, try to look ahead a little bit. For instance, our first word is three syllables. Officially, a word can have only one stress—we say "**re**-cent-ly," not "**re**-cent-**ly**"—though as you know by now, the rules loosen when we enter the spoken zone. (A little advance peek: When Maxi Jazz sings the word, he stresses the "ly" even though it's technically incorrect grammatically. There's no such thing as "incorrect" in oral performance; there's only "sounds good" and "doesn't.")

In any case, we're dealing with the word in print for now, and so I decided to scan it the way you see above—the way it's read traditionally.

The syllables that follow are more or less iambic if you look at them this way:

-ly **Ma**-ma's **cry**-ing **all** the **time**

3 **is it** be-**cause** of **me** or my **young**-er **sis**-ter,

This one's tough. "Is" and "it" seem to have equal weight to my ear. We could stress them both—or stress neither. (Stressing neither means, when spoken out loud, you more or less rush through those syllables on your way to the syllable that does get emphasis.) I decided to stress both because they're the first words of the line and probably get some attention.

"Be-cause" I stressed the way we pronounce this word traditionally.

The next syllable units are not easy to figure out. Prepositions like "of" rarely get emphasis, and, meaning-wise, the point of the clause seems to be "is it because of **me**?" so that's why I went with "of **me**." But by that logic, we would scan the next two syllables "or **my**." And that may be right. But to my ear, the line rushes through "or my" before laying the stress on "young" in "younger." (Both "**young**-er" and "**sis**-ter" are somewhat "easier" because we scan them the way they're pronounced out loud. It's in sequences of single syllables that things get a little tougher.) It's a toss-up.

This line gives us a poetry tutorial:

- Two equally stressed syllables in a row ("**is it**") are known as a **spondee**.
- "Be-**cause**" is an **iamb**—unstressed syllable followed by stressed.
- Same for "of **me**."
- We have something different next: Two unstressed syllables followed by one stressed. That's known as an **anapest**.
- We conclude with two **trochees**—units of a stressed syllable followed by unstressed. (The reverse of an iamb.)

4 e-ven **Dad** was **weep**-ing **when** he **kissed** her.

This line seems to follow a pretty consistent pattern, only that the stressed syllables come before unstressed: DUM-da, DUM-da, DUM-da, DUM-da, DUM-da. So we have five **trochees** in a row: **trochaic pentameter**.

5 **Face** all **puff**-y **like** a **blis**-ter,

More trochees, only there are four in this line: **trochaic tetrameter**. You may be wondering when to stress the first syllable of a line, and when the second. In the previous line, the answer was a little simpler: in the word "e-ven," it's the first syllable that gets stressed.

Here, the choice is between "face" and "all." (You may also be wondering why in some lines, like Line 3, the choice of what to stress isn't *between* the first two syllables, but between the first three or so. That's because those first two syllables—"is it"—are less "meaty," for lack of a better word, than syllables/words like "face" and "all." Just say out loud a sentence like "Is it your face?" In most instances, your voice will naturally stress "face" more than "is" or "it." To really hear it, ask your mentor to record you—it'll be very obvious when you're not trying to make sense of it at the same time as you're pronouncing it.")

Anyway, "all," seems to me to be more of the "is" and "it" stripe—a kind of connector—whereas "face" is the meat of the syllable unit. I decided to stress that.

I stressed the first syllable in "puff-y" because that's the way it's pronounced.

With "like a" we have one of those more complex challenges: Emphasize both? Neither? Only one? Which? I could see emphasizing neither—in that case, the words are just rushed through, a kind of lead-up to "blis-ter" (the way "or my" was before "young-er sis-ter." But "or my" were of equal length—they almost begged to be treated the same way. "Like" has four times as many letters as "a"). Also, when I say the words out loud—and that's what I had to do here, over and over, trying to slap the table in unison, to figure out what sounded the most natural—"like" seems to want the stress. The "like" seems more significant, meaning-wise, than "a"—"is it *like* or *unlike* a blister?" seems to be a more important question for the line than "is it like *a* blister or *the* blister?" (Can you see the degree of detail scansion gets into?! But it's not contrived; we are merely putting into words the processes our brains already go through in listening to a line of poetry, only without us realizing it.)

Finally, when we pronounce things out loud, we seek consistent alternations of stressed and unstressed syllables. As the poet Mary Oliver and others have pointed out, 10 syllables is the approximate length of the human breath, and the iamb is the most natural meter because it mimics the beat of our hearts: da-DUM, da-DUM, da-DUM, da-DUM, da-DUM. Hence iambic pentameter might be called the most natural poetic meter. Trochaic pentameter—DUM-da, DUM-da, DUM-da, DUM-da, DUM-da—isn't far behind. So I think I wanted to stress "like" because that made the line trochaic.

It may be frustrating that different "rules" seem to apply to a unit like "or my" in Line 3 and a unit like "like a" here. But I want to emphasize once more that these are **not** rules. There are good reasons, in many lines, to scan them in different ways, especially if we're reading the lines to ourselves rather than hearing them read out loud by the author or the singer, in Maxi Jazz's case. (I assure you that after you've listened to Maxi Jazz perform the lines, there will be absolutely no hesitation on your part about how to scan the lines. Though even then, that's not the "correct" version—merely Maxi Jazz's.)

Going back to the line: "Blis-ter," like "puff-y," is stressed the way it's pronounced. One "backdoor" way to figuring out the stress in a line of poetry is to start out by scanning multi-syllable words. Things may work differently in performance out-loud, but chances are that on the page, "blis-ter" will always be "**blis**-ter" rather than "blis-**ter**." That may help you figure out whether the syllables before and after it get stressed or not.

A final note: in this exercise we have song lyrics rather than a poem set to music. Poems tend to be far tighter in meter than songs. For instance, you'll almost never see three unstressed syllables in a row, the way you do in one scansion of Line 20. ("But she **know** I want my **Dad** I want my **fam**-i-ly **back**.") Written poetry is more "regular" than this because it needs the music of the line far more than a song, since a song has help from instruments and poetry has only the sound of the words.

Can you do the rest? Find my scansion of these lines at the end of the exercise, but please remember that this is only one way to do things.

6 cry-ing like he missed her.
7 Since we moved a-way from the house,
8 where we used to play.
9 They say I'll un-der-stand one day but I doubt it,
10 Ma-ma nev-er say noth-ing a-bout it.
11 How'd it get to be so crowd-ed.
12 I found it a strain, eve-ry-where I look I see pain.
13 And I can't es-cape the feel-ing,
14 may-be I'm to blame. So I strain to lis-ten,
15 Pray-ing for a de-ci-sion, wish-ing they were kiss-ing.
16 This feels like ex-tra-di-tion or ex-ile,
17 Ma-ma finds it hard to smile
18 So I make pre-tend cups of cof-fee in her fa-vor-ite style.

19 She says child I'm work-ing so there's noth-ing you lack.
20 But she know I want my Dad I want my fam-i-ly back.

Your assignment, Part 2:

In the second part of the exercise, we'll revisit the opening lines to "Bring My Family Back" as a sound object.

Start by finding a version of the song on YouTube (there are many variations). Listen to the first verse **only**—through the line "I want my Dad, I want my family back"—several times. It's quite catchy and the words will stick in your mind quickly. Does it sound differently than you anticipated?

Next, break up the song lyrics (see #1 above) into lines *according to Maxi Jazz's performance of them*. (This'll be fairly easy because if you listen closely, he takes a quick breath at each new line.) My own attempt is provided at the end of this lesson—don't look at it until you try your hand.

My answer to the fourth exercise in Part 1: scansion

6 **cry**-ing **like** he **missed** her.
7 **Since** we **moved** a-**way from** the **house**,
8 **where** we **used** to **play**.
9 **They** say **I'll** un-der-**stand** one **day** but I **doubt** it,
10 **Ma**-ma **nev**-er **say noth**-ing a-**bout** it.
11 **How'd** it **get** to **be** so **crowd**-ed.
12 I **found** it a **strain**, **eve**-ry-where **I** look I see **pain**.
13 And **I can't** es-**cape** the **feel**-ing,
14 **may**-be **I'm** to **blame**. **So** I **strain** to **lis**-ten,
15 **Pray**-ing **for** a de-**ci**-sion, **wish**-ing **they** were **kiss**-ing.
16 This **feels** like ex-tra-**di**-tion or **ex**-ile,
17 **Ma**-ma **finds** it **hard** to **smile**
18 So I **make** pre-**tend cups** of **cof**-fee in her **fa**-vor-ite **style**.
19 **She** says **child** I'm **work**-ing so there's **noth**-ing you **lack**.
20 But she **know** I want my **Dad** I want my **fam**-i-ly **back**.

My answer to Part 2:

1 I'm on lone-ly street
2 age near-ly three re-cent-ly
3 Ma-ma's cry-ing all the time is it be-cause of me

4 or my young-er sis-ter

5 even Dad was weep-ing when he kissed her.

6 Face all puff-y like a blis-ter,

7 cry-ing like he missed her.

8 Since we moved a-way from the house where we used to play they say I'll un-der-stand

9 one day

10 but I doubt it,

11 Ma-ma nev-er say noth-ing a-bout it

12 How'd it get to be so crowd-ed I found it a strain,

13 eve-ry-where I look I see pain

14 And I can't

15 es-cape the feel-ing may-be

16 I'm to blame. So I strain to lis-ten

17 Pray-ing for a de-ci-sion, wish-ing

18 they were kiss-ing. This feels like ex-tra-di-tion or ex-ile,

19 Ma-ma finds it hard to smile So I make pre-tend cups of cof-fee in her fa-vor-ite
style 20 She says

21 child I'm work-ing so there's noth-ing you lack.

22 But she know

23 I want my Dad I want my fam-i-ly back.

CHALLENGE EXERCISE:

1. Can you re-scan the lyrics according to what Maxi Jazz emphasizes in his
performance?

LISTENING TO THE WORLD

Purpose: To find material in the words around us.

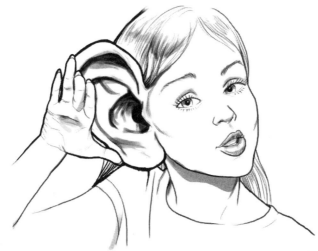

In Level One of this series, I asked you to listen to the world around you for a full week. You collected 20 snippets of dialogue, and then organized them into a poem of "glorious nonsense."

This week, we'll do something similar, but with a different purpose.

A poet must have the ear of a musician, picking up the finest distinctions in what the world sounds like, because it is that world that the poet tries to re-create in his work. This week, I want you to listen to the world around you: Listen to the conversation at dinner, to the news, to the radio, to conversations in the places where you find yourself—whether the grocery store line, swim practice, or a party. Pay particular attention to the talk that usually makes for background noise.

Whenever you hear a line that strikes you as intriguing, or interesting, or just pretty to your ear, write it down. Try to collect at least 15-20 individual lines. More is fine.

How will you know that something is worth recording? You'll know. Recently, I was playing a game called Library with some friends. In short, a player holds up a book, showing the others only the title. Based on that title, the players have to imagine what the first line of such a novel might be. In response to one of the novels—I forget which—one of the players came up with: "I am my father's bitter miracle." You have to agree that's a beautiful line. Why? I'm not sure; not every bit of beauty can be explained logically. But it's strange and unique and certainly makes me want to find out more. That's the kind of distinctive speech I want you to look out for this week.

Your assignment: At the end of the week, sort through the lines you've collected. Choose 10 and assemble them into a poem. It doesn't have to make complete sense, but try to keep the poem moving forward.

Below find 10 lines I collected throughout a week, to do the same exercise myself.

1. I am my father's bitter miracle
2. A flock of crows startled
3. No mice again
4. Longitudinal
5. Needle-eyed
6. There are three ways to tell if someone is lying
7. The sound stayed in her bones
8. The wooden palisades that kept the huskies in
9. Bore a hole in Mother's heart
10. King of the jungle, I felt that way

Your turn.

CHALLENGE EXERCISE:

Don't stop there. Go further with one of the 10 lines, building an entirely new poem around it.

FORMS

VILLANELLE

Purpose: To take our study of patterned poetry further.

In the previous section, you refreshed your familiarity with the patterns of repeated sounds and words; rhymes; syllables, and accents. This week, we take our understanding of patterns further by practicing what's known as **fixed verse**.

Throughout history, experiments with poetry have led to the creation of certain patterns that have become fixed—accepted and used by many poets. One such pattern is the **villanelle**.

In a villanelle:

- the first and third lines of the first stanza rhyme
- those two lines appear, taking turns, as the third line in every stanza that follows
- they also form the couplet that closes the villanelle
- villanelles are 19 lines long, consisting of five **tercets** (stanzas of the three lines) and one concluding **quatrain** (stanza of four lines)
- because of the above, villanelles have only two rhyme sounds

Put another way, a villanelle looks like this:

- The first and third lines of the first stanza rhyme:

Line 1 [A]
Line 2 [B]
Line 3 [A]

- They appear, taking turns, as the third line in every stanza that follows:

  Line 4 [A]
  Line 5 [B]
  Line 6, or 1 [A]

  Line 7 [A]
  Line 8 [B]
  Line 9, or 3 [A]

  Line 10 [A]
  Line 11 [B]
  Line 12, or 1 [A]

  Line 13 [A]
  Line 14 [B]
  Line 15, or 3 [A]

  Line 16 [A]
  Line 17 [B]

- They also form the couplet that closes the villanelle:

  Line 1 [A]
  Line 3 [B]

Here's an example of a villanelle, by Edwin Arlington Robinson:

The House on the Hill

They are all gone away,
The House is shut and still,
There is nothing more to say.

Through broken walls and gray
The winds blow bleak and shrill.
They are all gone away.

Nor is there one to-day

To speak them good or ill:
There is nothing more to say.

Why is it then we stray
Around the sunken sill?
They are all gone away,

And our poor fancy-play
For them is wasted skill:
There is nothing more to say.

There is ruin and decay
In the House on the Hill:
They are all gone away,
There is nothing more to say.[50]

What did you think? Doesn't the repetition create a powerful, chant-like effect?

Your assignment: Write your own villanelle.

How to do it? The good news is that the poem is half-written when you come up with the first stanza, since two out of its three lines will repeat throughout the poem. So that's where your focus should be. Forget for the moment about the rules that apply to the stanzas that follow.

Hint: For all three lines of the first stanza, you'll want to pick words that are easy to rhyme because so many words in the poem will need to rhyme with them. To write three brand-new lines *and* rhyme them is a tall order all at once, so separate the tasks. Start by putting down three lines—without rhyme if need be. Then you can tweak them to see if you can make the first and third rhyme while still making sense.

50   Edwin Arlington Robinson, *The Torrent and The Night Before.* (Cambridge, MA: Riverside Press, 1896), p. 13.

The poem doesn't have to be as grave as Robinson's, or as grandiose as some of the poems you've read this semester; if it feels easier to do something comic or nonsensical, go for it:

> So now he wants a villanelle
> As if I were a scholar of some kind
> But I barely know how to spell,
>
> And prefer to gambol in the dell
> While chewing on an orange rind.
> But now he wants a villanelle.

Note the way I slightly modified the first line when it appears as the third line in the second stanza. It's okay to do that if it makes life easier and helps the poem make sense. You're welcome to write something nonsensical, as I said, but the goal should be to make sense if possible. (Note as well the slight difference in both ring and meaning that the first line of the poem has when it appears again, as the third line of the next stanza.)

Once I had come up with the first stanza, I limited myself to thinking of the first line of the second stanza. I knew it had to rhyme with the first and third lines of the first, and I had taken care to give myself a common rhyme sound ("–elle"). I drew up a short list of words that rhyme with "–elle"—"sell," "dwell," "quell"—and when I wrote "dell," my mind hit on the idea for the line you see. I did the same thing with the second lines—first I tried to give myself a common rhyme to work with ("kind"), then wrote a list of words that rhyme—"signed," "bind," "wind"—and decided to go semi-nonsensical with "rind."

You might ask: "What's the purpose of doing exercises like this? Isn't it just a contrivance to give us something to do?" Yes and no. Exercises like this teach the incredible effect of patterning and repetition in poetry, which, as the lesson from two weeks ago reminded us, is, at its heart, music. For your next poem, you may not write a villanelle, but its echo patterns may influence the poem you do write. Secondly, this kind of exercise, plainly, can be fun. But thirdly, the restrictions it imposes force you to think harder for answers. And while your poem about chewing orange rinds in the dell instead of writing an assigned villanelle may not lead to publication, it will be great practice for your wits, your rhyming skills, and your general poetry knowledge.

Your turn. Get to work on your villanelle. You can choose whether to use the same meter throughout, or whether to let your lines be of different lengths with different rhythms. Your main focus needs to be on those repeated lines and rhymes, and on fitting them into the overall meaning of the poem.

CHALLENGE EXERCISE:

The **pantoum** is a relative of the villanelle in that certain rhymes repeat throughout the poem. As opposed to a villanelle, which proceeds in tercets, a pantoum does so in quatrains, or four-line stanzas. The repeating pattern is this:

• The second and fourth lines of each stanza repeat as the first and third lines of the next stanza.

That is, it isn't lines from the first stanza that repeat over and over; rather, lines from each stanza repeat once.

Pantoums also don't have a specific number of stanzas, the way villanelles do, though four are most common.

Finally, lines 2 and 4 of the last stanza don't repeat because the poem is over.

Here's a pantoum in visual form, followed by a pantoum by Charles Baudelaire, the great French poet, in the original French, so you can see the pattern without being distracted by meaning (unless you know French, of course).

A
B
C
D

B
E
D
F

E
G

F
H

G
I
H
J

Harmonie du soir

Voici venir les temps où vibrant sur sa tige

Chaque fleur s'évapore ainsi qu'un encensoir;

Les sons et les parfums tournent dans l'air du soir;

Valse mélancolique et langoureux vertige!

Chaque fleur s'évapore ainsi qu'un encensoir;

Le violon frémit comme un coeur qu'on afflige;

Valse mélancolique et langoureux vertige!

Le ciel est triste et beau comme un grand reposoir.

Le violon frémit comme un coeur qu'on afflige,

Un coeur tendre, qui hait le néant vaste et noir!

Le ciel est triste et beau comme un grand reposoir;

Le soleil s'est noyé dans son sang qui se fige.

Un coeur tendre, qui hait le néant vaste et noir,

Du passé lumineux recueille tout vestige!

Le soleil s'est noyé dans son sang qui se fige...

Ton souvenir en moi luit comme un ostensoir![51]

Your **challenge exercise** this week is to try a pantoum of your own.

51 Baudelaire, Charles. *Fleurs du Mal.* (Paris, France: Michel Levy Freres, 1868), p. 155.

SESTINA

Purpose: To continue our study of fixed verse.

A sestina is a more ambitious undertaking than either a villanelle (19 lines) or a pantoum (often 16 lines), both because it's longer (39 lines) and its pattern is even more elaborate, if you can believe it. Let's do things differently this week and start things off with a sestina entitled, appropriately, "Sestina," by Edmund Gosse.

Your assignment: Having read it, can you figure out what the pattern is?

Sestina
by Edmund Gosse

TO F. H.

'Fra tutti il primo Arnaldo Daniello[52]
Gran maestro d' amor.'–Petrarch.

In fair Provence, the land of lute and rose,
Arnaut, great master of the lore of love,
First wrought sestines to win his lady's heart,
For she was deaf when simpler staves he sang,

---

[52] The French mathematician and troubadour Arnaut Daniel, mentioned in the epigraph and in the poem itself, is said to have invented the sestina in the 12th century.

And for her sake he broke the bonds of rhyme,
And in this subtler measure hid his woe.

'Harsh be my lines,' cried Arnaut, 'harsh the woe
My lady, that enthorn'd and cruel rose,
Inflicts on him that made her live in rhyme!'
But through the metre spake the voice of Love,
And like a wild-wood nightingale he sang
Who thought in crabbed lays to ease his heart.

It is not told if her untoward heart
Was melted by her poet's lyric woe,
Or if in vain so amorously he sang;
Perchance through cloud of dark conceits he rose
To nobler heights of philosophic song,
And crowned his later years with sterner rhyme.

This thing alone we know: the triple rhyme
Of him who bared his vast and passionate heart
To all the crossing flames of hate and love,
Wears in the midst of all its storm of woe,---
As some loud morn of March may bear a rose,---
The impress of a song that Arnaut sang.

'Smith of his mother-tongue,' the Frenchman sang
Of Lancelot and of Galahad, the rhyme
That beat so bloodlike at its core of rose,
It stirred the sweet Francesca's gentle heart
To take that kiss that brought her so much woe
And sealed in fire her martyrdom of love.

And Dante, full of her immortal love,
Stayed his drear song, and softly, fondly sang
As though his voice broke with that weight of woe;
And to this day we think of Arnaut's rhyme
Whenever pity at the labouring heart
On fair Francesca's memory drops the rose.

Ah! sovereign Love, forgive this weaker rhyme!
The men of old who sang were great at heart,
Yet have we too known woe, and worn thy rose.[53]

There are several key qualities to a sestina. I'll prompt you with questions:

1. How many stanzas of how many lines does a sestina have?
2. Do any of its lines repeat?
3. How about any words?
4. What's the rhyme scheme—better called the repeat-scheme—of the poem?

Your answers:

1. _____

2. _____

3. _____

4. _____

Answers:

1. Six stanzas of six lines each, and a concluding tercet
2. No
3. Yes. One of the same six words concludes each of the sestina's 39 lines.
4. Repeat scheme:

Let's tackle this one together. In the first stanza, none of the lines rhyme/repeat:

In fair Provence, the land of lute and rose,	A
Arnaut, great master of the lore of love,	B
First wrought sestines to win his lady's heart,	C
For she was deaf when simpler staves he sang,	D

53   Gosse, Edmund. *New Poems*. (London: C. Kegan Paul & Co., 1879). pp. 157-59

And for her sake he broke the bonds of rhyme,	E
And in this subtler measure hid his woe.	F

In the second stanza, each line ends with the same words as the lines in the first stanza, only in a different order:

'Harsh be my lines,' cried Arnaut, 'harsh the woe	F
My lady, that enthorn'd and cruel rose,	A
Inflicts on him that made her live in rhyme!'	E
But through the metre spake the voice of Love,	B
And like a wild-wood nightingale he sang	D
Who thought in crabbed lays to ease his heart.	C

Can you finish the rhyme scheme out?

What did you come up with? For the answer, see the bottom of the page.

The sestina is a tough form, and this week, I only wanted you to become acquainted with its basics through Gosse's famous example. But if you want to take a stab at your own, that will be this week's **challenge exercise**.

Answer:

Stanza 1: ABCDEF
Stanza 2: FAEBDC
Stanza 3: CFDABE
Stanza 4: ECBFAD
Stanza 5: DEACFB
Stanza 6: BDFECA
Concluding tercet: ECA (can be ACE as well)

NONSENSE

ERASURE POETRY

Purpose: To create absurdity from perfectly sensible poems.

Last year, we talked about the value of nonsense in poetry. To refresh: Poetry that doesn't stress rational meaning often allows sound to take center-stage (a great example of this is "Jabberwocky" by Lewis Carroll, from Week 7). Or, more simply, nonsense poems stress a different kind of meaning. This "meaning" may be harder to describe, but it's meaning all the same. Think back to our "experimental fiction" lesson in the fiction section, specifically to Daniil Kharms's mini-story about the falling grandmothers. We could tease all kinds of "deep" meaning out of it: It's a story about the cruelty of the world, its brevity only underscoring the cold-heartedness of its demeanor. Or you can do a less literal read: The story is strange, and not quite explicable, but quite funny, and, in the end, delightful for reasons that are hard to explain.

Nonsense in poetry goes after the same effects. Even more than fiction, poetry deals with delight, surprise, fresh kinds of perception, new ways of saying things—you could call it the "ah" moment.

Next week, we'll study experimental poetry by masters of the genre, but this week, we'll be masters of the genre ourselves and practice it on our own through erasure poetry. Erasure poetry does exactly what it sounds like—you take a perfectly sensible poem, and start striking out words, phrases, lines, whatever your pleasure. The aim is to create a new poem that connects some of the old version's words with each other in a new way. The result is delightful nonsense—or maybe not. It's one kind of challenge to turn sense into nonsense, and another to turn sense into a less literal kind of sense, but sense all the same.

So, for instance, a poem like "Fog," by Carl Sandburg, from Week 2—

The fog comes
on little cat feet.

It sits looking
over harbor and city
on silent haunches
and then moves on.

—might read like this:

The fog _x_
on little _x_ feet.

It _x_ looking
over _x_ and city
_x_ silent haunches
_x_ then moves _x_.
Let's read it without the x's:

The fog
on little feet.

It looking
over and city
silent haunches
then moves.

The first stanza actually works as if it's intentional, though, you'll notice, it says something different from the original. The second one is less successful—not because it doesn't "make sense," but because even in its absurdity, it's not very interesting, partly because it doesn't align grammatically. Part of the reason, I think, is that "Fog" is very short, so there isn't much to play with, but also that I cut out words without thinking about it. (You may have noticed that I simply took out every third word.) What if I tried to cut words, phrases, or lines in "Fog" with an eye toward a kind of nonsensical sense? Let's focus on the first stanza:

Original:
The fog comes
on little cat feet.

Alternatives:
The fog
on feet

Comes
little cat

The little cat feet

Stanza 2: [using "Comes/little cat" as the first]

Original:
It sits looking
over harbor and city
on silent haunches
and then moves on.

Alternatives:
looking
over harbor
silent
moves

sits
over city
silent

looking
over
silent
moves

And so on.

Your turn.

Your assignment: Pick a published poem we've dealt with this year, or one of your own. (Make sure it's a bit longer than "Fog.") Then erase words, phrases, lines, or even stanzas from it in order to create a new nonsensical poem from the remaining words. Because so many options are possible, create at least three new versions of the poem.

In at least one version, try to cut no more than one word per line, or a total of eight words in a stanza of eight lines. I ask this because it becomes quite easy to create a new poem if you can just keep deleting words until you hit on something workable. The ultimate challenge is to keep as many in there as possible while still making no sense. At the same time, you want to cut *at least* one word per line; otherwise you're left with a poem as sensible as the original.

In one other version, go for humor—try to make it as funny as you can.

In the third version, do whatever you want.

CHALLENGE EXERCISE:

Write an absurd poem from scratch.

IN THE FOOTSTEPS OF FEDERICO GARCÍA LORCA

Purpose: To familiarize ourselves with the Surrealists and other
experimental poets.

Last week, you created an absurd poem. This week, you'll get acquainted with poetic experimentation by published poets. We'll focus our discussion on the Surrealists, the artists, filmmakers, and writers who forged a new, apparently nonsensical kind of art in the 1920s. At the end of the lesson, after filling up on Surrealist poems, you'll attempt to write a poem in the Surrealist style—a preparation for next week's exercise, which asks you to read a dozen poems by the same poet and write a poem in that poet's style.

This week presents an additional opportunity to prepare for that lesson in that it focuses on the work of a particular Surrealist poet: Federico García Lorca. Lorca is perhaps Spain's greatest 20th century poet, tragically killed at the outset of the Spanish Civil War in 1936, when he was only 38. More about him below.

Surrealism grew out of Dadaism, an early-20th century artistic movement that aimed to do away with stateliness, decorum, and good manners in art. Dadaist artists produced works of irrationality and nonsense, ugliness and cynicism, intending to offend and mark a clear path away from "good taste." It was the "good taste" society, in their view, that had blundered the world into the horrors of World War I. The Dadaists started to look for the beautiful in the ugly and nonsensical because conventional standards and authority had been discredited.

The Surrealists came into being in the 1920s, when the world was beginning to recover from this experience. But Surrealism was, in its own way, a reaction to the war, too. Only the Surrealists didn't do battle with traditional art and its promises; they hoped to escape from reality altogether. Perhaps the most popular example of Surrealist art is the painting *The Persistence of Memory* by Salvador Dalí, featuring clocks melting over a tree branch, a ledge, and a mysterious creature.

To give you an idea of Surrealist poetry, here's a short poem by Federico García Lorca:

The Little Mute Boy
translated by W. S. Merwin

The little boy was looking for his voice.
(The king of the crickets had it.)
In a drop of water
the little boy was looking for his voice.

I do not want it for speaking with;
I will make a ring of it
so that he may wear my silence
on his little finger

In a drop of water
the little boy was looking for his voice.

(The captive voice, far away,
put on a cricket's clothes.) [54]

A boy who's lost his voice to the king of the crickets; who searches for it in a drop of water; a narrator who makes a ring from that voice so that the boy "may wear [his] silence"; and, finally, the voice gets dressed up in cricket clothes. This goes beyond metaphor! This is, well, Surrealism. But are the imagery and associations random, the imagination going wild, or is there order to the (apparent) madness?

---

54   From *The Selected Poems of Federico García Lorca,* by Federico García Lorca, translated by W.S. Merwin. (New York, NY: New Directions, 1955)

I think we can agree it's a non-rational poetry. But is it nonsensical? I'm not sure. Simply, the poems make a different kind of sense, one that emerges from the heart or soul or senses or something even more mysterious or difficult to pin down. Take the opening lines of a Lorca poem about New York:

City That Does Not Sleep
translated by Robert Bly

In the sky there is nobody asleep. Nobody, nobody.
Nobody is asleep. The creatures of the moon sniff and prowl about their cabins.
The living iguanas will come and bite the men who do not dream,
and the man who rushes out with his spirit broken will meet on the street corner
the unbelievable alligator quiet beneath the tender protest of the stars. [55]

Now, none of this "makes sense" in the traditional definition—I live in New York, and I can assure you I don't hear stars protesting, tenderly or not, nor alligators lining up beneath them. But I can just as confidently declare that in this crush of beautiful, mystical, otherworldly images, Lorca has definitely captured something of my city's strange energy.

55 "Ciudad sin sueno / City That Does Not Sleep" by Federico García Lorca. From *Obras Completas* (Galaxia/Gutenberg, 1996 edition). English Translation by Robert Bly copyright © Robert Bly and Herederos de Federico García Lorca. All rights reserved.

Think of Lorca's work as a kind of fantasy not unlike the fantasy fiction we dealt with in the fiction section earlier this year.

Your assignment this week is to try your hand at a surrealist poem. I hope you'll find the exercise liberating rather than stressful. Lorca didn't throw down the first thing that came to mind; his imagery, despite seeming random, is carefully selected to create the effect that it does. But it would be okay, in your first stab at this kind of poetry, to do a first draft of the first things that come to mind. Something really silly, like:

> The furnaces of the finger blast a wicked winter
> Silence rains onto the apple like a dunce

And so forth.

But in your second draft, you might try to craft this freewheeling nonsense into something that feels a bit less random. Is there anything in the two lines above that suggests a consistent direction, however non-rational that direction is?

Here's a clue to how the Surrealist mind—or the Surrealism-imitating mind—works. Even thought I threw down the first words that came to mind, you'll notice several of them have to do with weather: "furnaces," "winter," "rains." Not coincidentally, I wrote them while sitting in front of an open window, rain pouring outside and cold air blowing in. It's a great example of how the subconscious shapes our word choices even as we think we maintain rational control. (When I wrote the lines, I was feeling a bit cold, but was too occupied by the lesson to get up and close the window—perhaps that's why I ended up blurting out words about the weather.)

But more to the point, is there a way to improve what I've put down? In trying to answer, you might lean on the single-metaphor exercise from earlier this year. There, you had to develop a rich set of associations for the original component of the comparison. Similarly, here I might think a little bit more about those furnaces and rains:

> The gray milk of rain fills
> the silences left by the exiled sun

That is, you're trying to make *some* sense—only that you're using the most inventive, imaginative, non-realistic description possible. Typically, we don't think of the sun as leaving a "silence" behind. But in a less strict sense, when the sun disappears, whether because of bad weather or nightfall, doesn't that kind of quiet things down? The rain that's replaced the sun is gray and wet ("gray milk"), so gray and wet that it's hard to imagine the sun ever returning ("exiled").

Your assignment: Aim for a poem of 16 lines in length if you need a guideline. Go at the poem as many times as you need to in order to chisel from it something that retains a Lorca-like magic while also not seeming random. It's a difficult challenge, and you may not reach it this week. But go through as many drafts as you can.

CHALLENGE EXERCISE:

1. Read more Surrealist poetry. Below are the titles of four poems that epitomize the genre and should be easily findable online.

"The Absence," by Paul Eluard

"Salvador Dalí," by David Gascoyne

2. Read more Federico García Lorca. If you do, it can count toward your assignment next week. If you're not sure which translation to use, go for Lorca's *Selected Poems*, edited by Donald Allen and Federico's brother Francisco García Lorca (New Directions, 1955).

If that one proves hard to find, there are also:

The Collected Poems: A Bilingual Edition, edited by Christopher Maurer (2002)
Selected Poems, edited by Donald Allen and introduction by W. S. Merwin (2005)

3. Read another master of surpassingly imaginative poetry: Paul Celan. First, get an introduction to his life via Wikipedia or his biography page on Poets.org. Then, read at least two poems by him. Suggestions: First the short "O Little Root of a Dream." Then, the epic and famous "Death Fugue" (one of whose expressions I modified for one of my own "Surrealist" examples above. Can you spot what I took?)

POETRY · SECTION 6

FAVORITE POET

GETTING TO KNOW...

Purpose: To study a poet's work in more detail.

Over the course of this semester you've come into contact, perhaps not for the first time, with the work of more than a dozen poets:

Carl Sandburg
Walt Whitman
Alfred, Lord Tennyson
Emily Dickinson
Alexander Pushkin
Charles Baudelaire
Elizabeth Bishop
William Butler Yeats
Lewis Carroll
Edwin Arlington Robinson
Edmund Gosse
Federico García Lorca
Paul Celan

If you've worked with previous volumes of this series, you can add to this list:

Edgar Allan Poe
Robert Frost
Matthew Arnold
D. H. Lawrence
Oscar Wilde
William Wordsworth

James Joyce
William Blake
Matsuo Basho
Mary Oliver
Sharon Olds
C. K. Williams
John Donne
Joseph Hutchison
Rainer Maria Rilke

Did the work of any of these poets intrigue you enough to want to read more? If not, a list of some of history's greatest poets follows at the end of this lesson; Poets.org, the official website of the Academy of American Poets, provides wonderful thumbnails on each, including a sampling of their works.

Your assignment: Whomever you choose—and you may need to go through poems by a couple before you settle on one that really affects you—read at least a dozen poems by that poet. You may supplement your reading with some basics about his or her life. Don't get too detailed; you don't want to overwhelm your appreciation of the poetry with biographical information. The length of the biographical thumbnail on Poets.org is just perfect.

One thing that the bio thumbnail could be really useful for is a sense of the poet's evolution. In choosing the dozen poems, try to pick a selection that spans the poet's career so you can try to experience the evolution first-hand. (For example, Paul Celan, whom you met last week, wrote increasingly nonsensical, fragmented, and abstract poems as he got older.)

If the poet originally wrote in a foreign language, it might be fun to read a handful of the poems in the original, whether you speak it or not (make sure to read them aloud). Also, using a search engine, try to seek out more than one translation of a given poem, if it's been translated more than once.

As you read, think about the poet's style as much as you can, using the tools you've acquired this year and in years past. Ask yourself a handful of the following questions.

1. What are the poems about? Do you find a unifying theme/set of concerns?

2. What are some of the most dominant elements of the poem(s)? Rhyme? The singularity of the descriptions? A strict rhythm?

3. Say more about the dominant elements: How do they work?

4. Do the poems tend to tell stories, or are they primarily descriptive/sensory?

5. Who is speaking?

6. Does the poet have a message? Another way of asking this would be: What do you think the poet really cares about, in his or her work and life? Can you tell? Does the poet hammer this point, or address it more subtly?

7. Is there anything, stylistically, the poet seems to avoid?

8. How do comparisons work throughout the poem?

9. Are the stanzas regular or seemingly random?

10. Look at line endings: Do the lines end on complete sentences, or carry over?

11. What general feelings do the poems create: Speed, languor, melancholy, rage?

12. Who does the poet cite as influences? Can you look at several poems by each of those poets? Can you draw connections between them?

13. Imagine discussing the poem in question with the poet. What would you talk about?

14. Discuss the poem with your mentor.

15. Write an e-mail to a friend you think would like the poem, and explain why in the e-mail.

Jot down the answers to at least half of these questions, or explain your answers to your mentor.

CHALLENGE EXERCISE:

1. So far, we've cast our net broadly but shallowly: You've read no more than a handful of poems by any given poet. Now I want you to go narrow but deep, to get so closely acquainted with a poet's work that you begin to develop an instinct for its primary qualities, and a kinship with the poet him- or herself. This week's challenge exercise is to write a poem in the style—in conscious imitation of—that poet.

2. Re-type at least two poems by the poet in your own hand. How does it feel?

3. Take over my duties: Come up with an exercise based on this week's assignment, namely a close study of a poet's work.

In writing a poem in the style of the poet (**Challenge exercise 1**), you may wish to concentrate on the dominant aspects of that poet's work. For me, Federico García Lorca's otherworldly imagery is more pressing than the way he uses stanzas, or even sound. (At least as translated into English.) With Robert Frost, I pay attention to the rhyme and the plainspoken wisdom of what he's saying. With Celan, it's the general atmosphere of dread. (I am thinking especially of "Death Fugue.") With Walt Whitman, it's the atmosphere of exultation, of energy, of enthusiasm—all those exclamation marks raining down.

What does it mean to imitate this? You can write a poem full of exclamation marks that resembles Whitman only in some superficial sense, and you can write a poem without exclamation marks that captures the drive of his poems perfectly. Imitation isn't carbon-copying; I want you to be inspired by something in the poems; how you translate that into your work is your freedom—and challenge.

A great resource to aid you in this exercise is the anthology *Sleeping on the Wing: An Anthology of Modern Poetry with Essays on Reading and Writing*, edited by Kenneth Koch and Kate Farrell (Random House, 1982). It offers a selection of poems from more than 20 poets, along with introductions to their work and poetic sensibilities. Most importantly, it discusses what it might mean to write a poem in the style of, say,

Walt Whitman and Emily Dickinson. (See the essays that follow each poet's selection of poems.) For an example of the book's helpfulness, check out the authors' essay on Federico García Lorca, a poet you now have some familiarity with, on pages 210-13.

As promised, here's a list of other poets you'd do well to become acquainted with, grouped roughly by time period and geographic origin. This is my list, colored by my own experiences and preferences; there are certainly many other poets worth investigating.

John Keats
Alexander Pope
Elizabeth Barrett Browning
Percy Bysshe Shelley
Samuel Tayor Coleridge
Gerard Manley Hopkins
Dylan Thomas
T. S. Eliot
Ezra Pound
Edna St. Vincent Millay
Wallace Stevens
W. H. Auden
Gertrude Stein
Sylvia Plath
Robert Hayden
Gwendolyn Brooks
Theodore Roethke
Ted Hughes
Philip Larkin
Robert Lowell
Kenneth Koch
Allen Ginsberg
Adrienne Rich
Marianne Moore
Robert Hass
Robert Pinsky
John Ashbery
W. S. Merwin
Paul Muldoon

Seamus Heaney
Maya Angelou
Pablo Neruda (Chile; Spanish)
Octavio Paz (Mexico; Spanish)
Fernando Pessoa (Portuguese)
Arthur Rimbaud (French)
Osip Mandelstam (Russian)
Anna Akhmatova (Rusisan)
Marina Tsvetaeva (Russian)
Vladimir Mayakovsky (Russian)
Yevgeny Yevtushenko (Russian)
Joseph Brodsky (Russian, English)
Boris Pasternak (Russian)
Czeslaw Milosz (Polish)
Wislawa Szymborska (Polish)

CENTO

Purpose: To go further with our study of a poet's work by writing a new poem composed of lines from the poems you read last week.

Cento is Latin for "patchwork," or a cloak made of patches. Makes sense, then, that in poetry, *cento* refers to a poem made up of lines by other poets.

To see how this works, you might search for and read the following six poems online:

Charles Wright, "In the Kingdom of the Past, the Brown-Eyed Man is King"

Marie Ponsot, "One is One"

Emily Dickinson, "After great pain a formal feeling comes—"

Sylvia Plath, "The Hanging Man"

Charles Wright, "After Reading Tu Fu, I Go Outside to the Dwarf Orchard"

Samuel Beckett, "Cascando"

Now, check out the brief cento made from these poems by the staff of the Academy of American Poets, which runs the Poets.org website:

> In the Kingdom of the Past, the Brown-Eyed Man is King
> Brute. Spy. I trusted you. Now you reel & brawl.
> After great pain, a formal feeling comes—

A vulturous boredom pinned me in this tree
Day after day, I become of less use to myself,
The hours after you are gone are so leaden.[56]

The authors of the cento tried to make as much "sense" as possible with their collage of lines—they chose lines that seem to center, more or less, on the relations of two creatures. Since such experimental assignments lead to rather nonsensical poems by definition, trying to make as much sense *as possible* despite the limitation is a great way to find a balance.

Your assignment: This week, write your own *modified* cento. You won't be creating a collage of lines by other poets. Instead you'll be creating a collage of lines all by the same poet: the poet you studied last week. In this way, this exercise seeks to familiarize you even more closely with the poet's output.

Start by re-reading half of the poems you read by the author last week (Surely you liked some more than others? Pick those for re-reading.) Add to those a half-dozen new ones by the same poet.

Now you'll have read something like 20 poems by the poet in question. As you read, try to flag some lines that make you think of others in other poems by the same author. (Limit yourself to no more than two lines from the same poem.) The connection may be different in each case—treatment of the same subject, use of the same word, a certain kind of imagery. Don't think about it too much—trust your instincts. If you've read all the poems and still don't have enough lines flagged, go through them again.

The new poem you create could consist of a single stanza, or our default—four stanzas of four lines. But it might be more fun—and appropriate—to write the new poem in the shape of one of the poems by the author, say your favorite. For instance, two weeks ago we read "The Little Mute Boy," by Lorca. It has two stanzas of four lines apiece, and then two stanzas of two lines apiece. So, to get you started, I'll read several poems by Lorca in order to start a cento. I'll leave the first line from "The Little Mute Boy."

---

56   http://www.poets.org/viewmedia.php/prmMID/5771

The little boy was looking for his voice.

Next, I read a poem called "Arbolé, Arbolé" (available on Poets.org.) I read it focusing on one thing—a line that could go after what I've got above. I didn't have to go very far— the third line—before I found something that stuck out immediately: "The girl with the pretty face," a natural follow-on to a line about a boy. I finished reading the poem, though I didn't find anything that I wanted to add as the third line of my *cento*. So, now I have

The little boy was looking for his voice.
The girl with the pretty face

Moving on, I read "City That Does Not Sleep," excerpted two weeks ago. I wasn't sure what I was looking for—something squarely about boys and girls may have been too direct, too literal. Also, unlike the first line, which is a complete sentence, the second is not, so if I wanted to make a reasonable amount of sense, I needed to choose something that agreed with the sentence fragment in Line 2. Again, I didn't have to read far until I found something that seemed to "fit": "and the man who rushes out with his spirit broken will meet on the/street corner." And voila, I had my first four lines!

The little boy was looking for his voice.
The girl with the pretty face
and the man who rushes out with his spirit broken will meet on the
street corner.

Your turn.

CHALLENGE EXERCISE:

Create a cento of all the poets featured this year—it should be a far wilder result due to the fact that they come from such different eras and are, obviously, so much more different from each other than the works of a single writer.

ENLARGING OUR WORLD/POETRY AS A PUBLIC EXERCISE

POEM AS COLLEGE ESSAY

Purpose: To practice writing about ourselves for public consumption.

We're going to spend the two weeks of this section exploring the same idea in opposite ways. This week, you'll practice writing a personal poem for public consumption; next week, you'll write a poem about your moment in history. One assignment is inward-looking, the other as outward-looking as can be. But both ask you to engage with the world beyond your desk and home.

This week, your assignment is to write a poem about yourself. This probably sounds a lot easier than it actually is. What about myself? Here's one way to focus the exercise: If you'll be applying to college this or next year, consider writing a poem that you could submit in lieu of your personal essay. One thing I can guarantee is that it will make you stand out; those admissions counselors plow through thousands of personal essays, many of them dutiful and dry. But closer to our purposes, thinking of the assignment this way can help you shape the direction of the poem: What would I say, in poem form, to an admissions counselor whom I wanted to admit me to his or her college?

Your assignment, Part 1: Generate some ideas to get started, and get the basic words down on the page. What could such a poem be about? Well, the same things as your college essay:

- What I believe in
- What I wish for myself
- The most meaningful thing to have happened to me
- A painful lesson
- If I had a million dollars

- The meaning of family
- A great disappointment
- A friendship fallout
- The usefulness of negative feelings [Counselors love contrarian ideas]
- Favorite hobby
- My weaknesses/my fears

You don't have to write a catalog poem that mentions all of these categories, or a prose poem chopped up into lines of poetry. Focus on one or two themes and build them out. Say you choose "the usefulness of negative feelings." One option is to come up with a first line and see where it takes you:

Weakness is pain leaving the body, Father always said.

Or you could plan out the poem in advance:

A poem about negative feelings where the first stanza will describe negative experiences, like being bored or angry, as an opportunity to learn something; the second stanza…

In this approach, you plot out the message—in other words, you plan out what you're going to *explain*. This is like telling in fiction, and should be handled with extreme caution in poetry, because explaining/telling in poetry can quickly come to seem very didactic and boring. Even more than with fiction, the magic of poetry is in discovery.

Here's a third option: You might decide to focus the whole poem on an episode that ends up teaching you the value of negative experiences:

I'm going to tell the story of that time I hated being in camp, and every morning almost called home to be taken away. But some voice inside me said, 'Stay for now, you can always call tomorrow,' and I did. And while there were still plenty of boring or annoying days scattered between the decent ones, I learned the value of commitment.

This could be called the *showing* approach—you tell the story of an episode without meddling to explain *why* you're telling it, and then, perhaps in that last stanza that's going to resonate in people's minds, you hit the reader with a couple of lines that make clear what the experience meant to you.

Your assignment, Part 2:

After you've got the first draft down, return to the poem in order to work on some of its craft elements:

1. Read the poem out loud. Do any of the lines seem too long? Too short? You might wish to record yourself, or have a mentor listen, in order to be able to evaluate without having to concentrate on reading at the same time.

2. How about the stanzas? Do they have any regularity? Why or why not?

3. Review, microscopically, every phrase and word. Are any of them trite or redundant? Could you say what you're trying to say in fewer words?

4. Does the poem have a distinctive sound? Your poem doesn't have to rhyme like Faithless' "Bring My Family Back" in Week 8 or gorge on **alliteration** the way Walt Whitman's "Beat! Beat! Drums!" does in Week 7. But what you do does need to seem intentional and controlled rather than accidental. Remember the power of repetition as well. A poem where every line begins "If I had a million dollars…" makes a powerful impression on the reader. (It also sounds like a song.)

CHALLENGE EXERCISE:

Write a traditional college essay, and then chop it up into a poem.

THIS MOMENT IN HISTORY

Purpose: To appreciate the ways in which poetry has been used as a commentary on the political and identity issues of our time.

Last week, you took a step into the public eye by writing about yourself for public consumption. This week, you'll continue your work in the world beyond yourself by writing a poem about your moment in history. To understand what this might mean, let's look at a handful of poems that deal with issues larger than the self or interpersonal relations.

Look up some of these poems online:

> "Let America Be America Again," Langston Hughes
> "Theme for English B," Langston Hughes
> "I, Too, Sing America," Langston Hughes
> "America," Robert Creeley
> "Children of Our Era," Wislawa Szymborska
> "Election Year," Donald Revell
> "Four Preludes on Playthings of the Wind," Carl Sandburg
> "How We Did It," Muriel Rukeyser
> "Fellini in Purgatory," Jean Valentine

All these poems engage with issues of politics and identity: The Vietnam War, being black in America, sometimes simply the notion of hope in abstract (as in Donald Revell's poem). Some poems engage with the matter at hand quite directly (as Langston Hughes does), some less so (Wislawa Szymborska), some quite elliptically (Jean Valentine).

Your first decision is to decide what you want to discuss in your poem. Is it living in an age of climate change? Being a girl in the 21st century? America's place in the world? Your feelings about the rise of China? The shifts in gay marriage over the past decade?

Your next step is to focus this theme into a concrete jumping-off point for a poem. (If you happen to have Level Two of this series, revisit Week 4 in the Poetry section: From Themes to Situations.) Just like last week, you can write about a concrete episode that, in its details, ends up saying something about your larger point. Or you can dwell on the larger point directly. Or you can write a poem about something less literal, the way Donald Revell does.

In general, you should use this exercise as a dry run for the free exercise next week. Bring all the lessons you've learned about poetry this semester to bear on this directed assignment. I am instructing you what to write about; how you do it is up to you. However, this poem might make a fine pairing with your poem from last week as a submission in lieu of a college essay.

CHALLENGE EXERCISE:

Write a poem from the perspective, respectively, of a person of the other gender; a much older person; or someone of a different ethnic identity. This exercise combines this week's work with exercises you've done, in this and previous volumes, on point of view and climbing into the skin of a character unlike yourself, an essential skill for writers.

CONCLUSION

CLOSING POEM

Purpose: To practice without guidelines.

This week's exercise, as per tradition, asks you to write a poem without guidelines: about whatever you like, and however you like it. This year, we've focused a little bit less on *how* to write about something and more on *what* to write about, so you've had a good amount of practice coming up with subjects and writing about them the way that you'd like. This week's exercise concludes that pattern.

One of the upsides of writing so many poems in such a short period is the sense of regular practice it instills. As I'll describe in more detail in the essays in the appendix, daily practice—whether reading, brainstorming, or actually writing—is essential for a poet. One of the downsides of covering a new topic every week, however, is that it limits the amount of time one spends on a given poem. Few great poems get written in a week. They're labored over for far longer—a pace that might seem downright ancient in this sped-up world of ours (remember the poet Donald Hall from Week 6, who will revise the same poem hundreds of times). As many great poets will tell you, revision is even more important to a good poem than that first draft. (I wrote the first draft of my novel in nine months. I revised for more than two years afterward.)

All this is to say that this week, instead of writing a new poem, you might pick your favorite poem from the past 18 weeks and revise it. Maybe it's a poem you're drawn to but can't quite figure out how to improve; maybe it's something that came out too smoothly, and you'd like to revisit it; maybe it's something that seems to work perfectly well, but you'd like to take a closer look. (And if this is your first volume of *The Creative Writer* series, you might go back and re-do the assignment from Week 1 to measure your progress this year.)

Of course, you're free as well to try your hand at a brand-new poem. I only wanted to emphasize that the goal with poetry isn't volume so much as quality. Better to spend 18 weeks on a single great poem than to produce 18 merely decent ones.

No challenge exercise this week.

CONCLUDING THOUGHTS

This volume ends your study of writing in this format, but I hope it's only the beginning of regular writing practice in your life. As you enter college and the adult world, make room for reading and creative writing. That should be easier to do if you naturally enjoy it, but even if it comes with struggle, remember that a well-written sentence, be it in a short story or a legal brief or advertising copy, will always turn heads and win you admirers. Some of the skills we've been studying are particular to short stories and poems. But others—writing vividly, concisely, originally—are just as relevant for your college papers and summer-internship and job applications, not to mention the profession you choose after college.

Regular practice, as both a reader and writer, is the best way to nourish these skills. After practicing writing regularly for the last one to four years, I hope that it's become a habit—something you miss if you go a day or week without it. If that isn't the case, but you want writing to be a regular practice in your life all the same, establish a regular routine.

Discipline

<u>Writing</u>:

Choose two days a week—one weekday, one weekend—when you'll sit down to practice writing (using the exercises in this or previous volumes if you need to get your brain going). Block out the same hours—aim for 2-3—during your writing days. When is your mind freshest? I prefer to write in the morning, before the day has had a chance to intervene with unforeseen distractions. When planning for the week ahead, think of these blocks of time as spoken-for and non-negotiable. Only by regarding them as such will it be possible to make regular practice of them.

<u>Reading</u>:

Reading is just as important as writing. You should try to make time to read fiction or poetry daily, even if it's for only a half-hour. (It's better to read less every day than more once in a while.) You could skip reading on the days you write so it all doesn't take too much time, but try to make it as regular a practice as the writing. It may be difficult because you will have so much assigned reading in college. And if your course assignments include literature, those could sub for your daily allotment. But if not, reading a short story or poetry feeds a different part of the brain than reading a biochemistry textbook. Make time for it.

Community

One of the most useful things I did for my writing was to sign up for creative-writing classes in college and, afterward, to apply for a Master's program in fiction. Not only because of what I learned, but because it provided structure, discipline, and community. Suddenly, I wasn't alone in my room trying to motivate myself to write—I was part of a group whose members were all in the same boat. We could talk to each other about the excitements and challenges of what we were trying to do. We had deadlines. We learned in a structured way.

If your schedule allows for creative-writing classes and you have the interest, sign up. That you've been practicing using these volumes for at least a year should make you a very attractive candidate. If your schedule doesn't have the room or your college doesn't offer creative-writing classes, seek out other venues. Is there a literary magazine based at your college? Perhaps the campus newspaper features creative writing from time to time? Or perhaps there's some kind of outlet in the community where the college is located? Stop by the English Department and inquire. If anyone knows, its members do. If all else fails, start your own creative-writing workshop—one thing I can guarantee is that every campus will have quite a few souls who want to write fiction and poetry. It's a great way to make new friends, too.

Community doesn't have to be public. There are many online resources for budding writers, depending on whether you're looking for sample lessons or online-workshop communities. Typing something as simple as "online resources for young fiction writers" into a search engine brings up enough options to keep you busy for a long time.

Observation

As I've mentioned throughout our work together, a true writer writes regularly, reads regularly, and observes with a writer's eye at all times. As you move through life, keep an eye and ear peeled for the details that make for good fiction and poetry: distinctive speech, the unexpected details that affirm something as authentic, what motivates people to do what they do. Keep a small observation notebook in your pocket at all times, whether you're going to class or a party. Consider nothing too minor to note. Don't leave it till the morning if you've thought of something interesting on the verge of falling asleep. Many of these observations may not find their way into your writing immediately—though many will eventually, trust me on that—but they *will* help keep your writing skills sharply honed.

Submitting to a literary journal:

As I mentioned in my opening comments, it might be rewarding for you to submit a short story or poem for consideration by a literary magazine. Literary magazines typically publish fiction, nonfiction, and poetry, and are often supported financially by universities or foundations. As a result, they're less worried about the bottom line and often take chances on new and adventurous work. There are a great number out there and the single best way to find out about them is to head to the library and look up either the *2013 Novel & Short Story Writer's Market* or the *2013 Poet's Market* (both published by Writer's Digest Books).

Both volumes open with helpful essays on both craft and getting published. For instance, in the *2013 Novel & Short Story Writer's Market*, the literary agent Donald Maass weighs in on how writers go about "Crafting Emotion" and the editor Chuck Sambuchino writes about "Emerging Voices" (that would be you). In the *2013 Poet's Market*, you'll find essays on some of the same craft concepts we've covered, such as experimental poems and prose poems; it may be interesting for you to compare the instruction there with what you read in this series. Even more significantly, however, both books also feature long lists of literary magazines, replete with addresses, procedures for submission, submission fees (not exorbitant, usually), and so forth.

How to pick one? You might start with a local publication. Someone from nearby may be naturally interested in your work, especially if it touches on something local.

By the same logic, if your short story concerns North Dakota, see if there are literary magazines in North Dakota. (There are.)

Also, aim small to start. The *Novel & Short Story* book lists not only "literary magazines," but also "small circulation magazines." The smaller the magazine, the likelier it is that you will find a sympathetic, close reading. By a similar logic, focus as well on those magazines that specialize in publishing new voices.

If the publication's submission guidelines don't prohibit it, you may wish to submit a letter along with your short story or poem, explaining what brought you to submit this particular work to this particular publication. (You could mention your work with this series and then describe the work you're submitting.) Or you may wish to submit anonymously, relying on the quality of your submission and nothing more.

However—and this is important—don't submit something that hasn't been polished to the best of your ability (three drafts minimum) and been work-shopped among your mentor and friends. As I'll explain in more detail in the next paragraph, getting published by a literary magazine is *really, really* hard. Lit mags receive hundreds of submissions for every story or poem they're able to publish. You should send only your best.

After you mail off your story or poem, the best thing you can do is forget that you did so. Unsolicited submissions—that is, submissions the publication hasn't asked for—end up in something called a slush pile. These magazines are committed to reviewing every work that comes their way, but so many do that it often takes them months to respond. I know writers who've heard back in six weeks, and I know writers who've heard back in two years. Waiting for either is brutal; try to forget that you sent something out and be pleasantly surprised when you get a letter in the mail.

Chances are you *won't be* pleasantly surprised, however, because the letter is likely to include a rejection slip. Not because your poem is bad—99% of the stuff that comes a literary magazine's way will get rejected, either because the magazine can publish only so much; or because its staff liked the poem but it falls outside the scope of what the magazine usually publishes, either for reasons of form or content; or because, let's be honest, the poem isn't there just yet. The silliest thing you can do at this point is get discouraged. *Everybody*, even legends, start out by hearing *No*. I heard *No* twenty times before someone said *Yes*. And now that I hear *Yes* more often, I still hear *No* all the time. It's an unavoidable part of the game, and you know what? It makes you stronger. I was a far more fragile writer before I started hearing those *Nos*. I was also a lot less confident in my work. Hearing *No* and having to decide whether to dust myself off and try again forced me to have that much more faith in my writing: I had to believe in it more and more each time I got up and dusted.

One other important thing: Writers always assume that their rejections come from people who took a tremendous amount of time to evaluate their stories and poems. Not so. Many people who consider writing, whether for literary magazines or for review in book-review sections, don't take very close looks at the work, believe it or not. In other circumstances, their judgment simply isn't very good. One need look no further than the contrasting reviews the same movie or book will get in two different newspapers to understand that judgment of quality is very subjective.

So, don't get discouraged! Dust yourself off, and try again. And most importantly, keep writing.

The mentor has a critical, if changed, role to play as the writer moves from the firm structure of this learning format to the college environment. A writer benefits so much from a sounding board—someone with whom to discuss a particular character, or a story idea, or a rhyme; someone trustworthy to review a first draft; someone with whom to perform an exercise such as dialogue, which requires two people. Just as critically, you're the writer's connection to the last time he or she had regular writing practice, through this series. So that when the young writer's discipline begins to flag, you're ideally suited to step in and recommend some exercises—some of which you may enjoy doing alongside the young writer.

You have a careful balancing act to maintain in that the young writer ought to be encouraged to keep up a writing practice that may seem occasionally onerous, while being set free to explore her interest in writing on her own terms. You could help create structure by working out a plan with the writer for weekly writing and reading practice: these hours, in this place, with these goals. You could even create a plan for the entire school year, too: this many books or short stories read, this many short stories attempted, something similar for both reading and writing of poems, all progress marked in a journal to create a sense of momentum. You may wish to join the writer for some of the reading—a great way to stay in contact and a subject for bonding when she's away from home. This kind of plan can recreate the structure—the goals and deadlines—of a formal curriculum like this one.

Also, talk to the writer, not only about what he or she's read or attempted to write, but about what he or she has seen and noticed in the world. It's another, less formal occasion to connect over something larger than homework or daily doings. For instance, in my novel, I have a character from Germany who lives in New York. He decides to settle on the Upper East Side because its northern end, formerly known as Yorkville, used to be home to many German immigrants, and several establishments—a butcher, a bakery—survive from that time. Just the other day, however, I was having lunch with a friend from Spain who had just moved to New York. I asked her if she'd been to any of the Spanish restaurants in town. "Spanish restaurants in New York?" she said. "I get plenty of that at home." It made me realize that my German character probably wouldn't have settled near Yorkville. Those who voluntarily leave their homelands for a spell in New York may wish to experience something new rather than something familiar.

I bring this up because it's the kind of observation/realization that I want the writer to make, but it's also something that you can bring to the writer's attention, if it reminds you of a story he or she wrote. This kind of attention and engagement should be very gratifying for the young writer. Writing isn't an easy profession, and, in a parent, a child's interest in it is as likely to inspire anxiety as often as pride. Even if you ultimately won't encourage the writer to pursue the creative arts as a profession, it will be of great meaning to have such interest from you in his or her work. A mentor is truly a writer's first friend. I couldn't have gotten to where I am without the ones I've been fortunate enough to have.

PERMISSIONS